Nancy Hogan
Frank Elo

Ferris State University

one-time
online
access
code
included

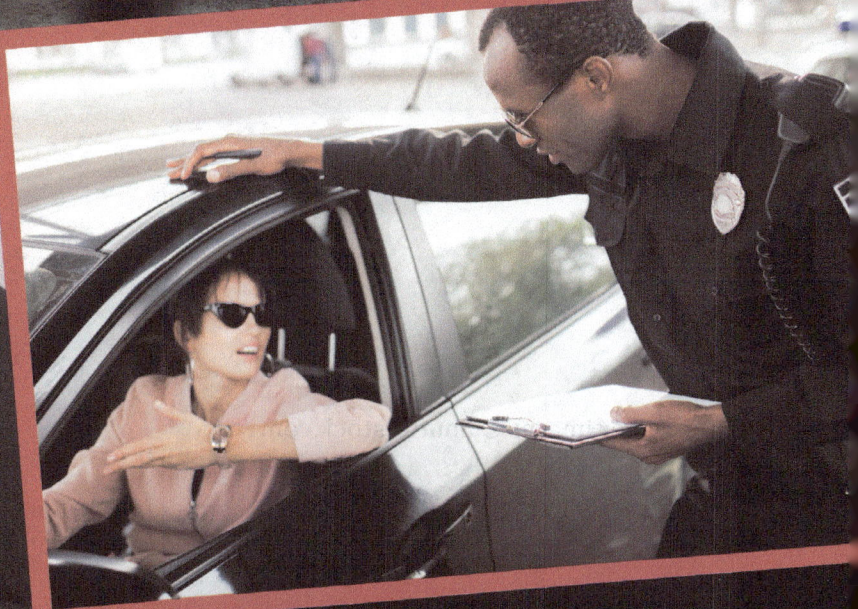

Kendall Hunt
publishing company

REPORT WRITING WORKBOOK
FOR CRIMINAL JUSTICE

Cover images © Shutterstock.com

Kendall Hunt
publishing company

www.kendallhunt.com
Send all inquiries to:
4050 Westmark Drive
Dubuque, IA 52004-1840

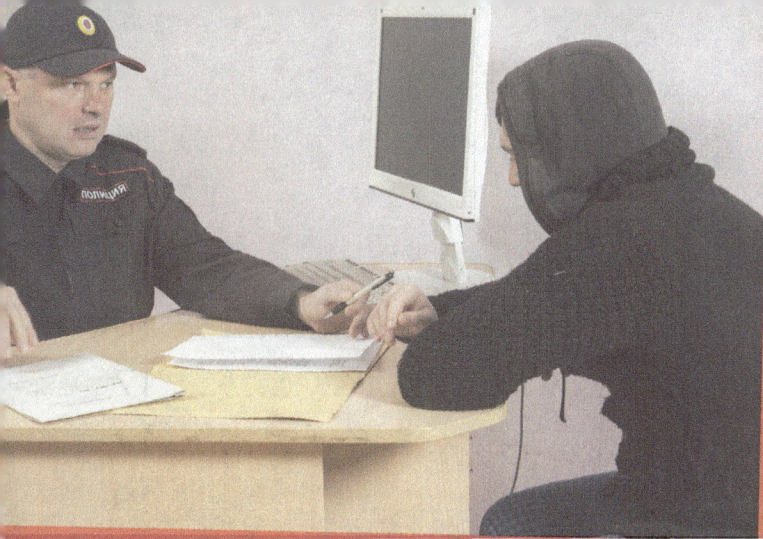

Contents

1 A Professional Attitude 1

    Reference 3

2 The Mechanics of Writing 5

    Capital Letters 5

    Writing Numbers 6

    Abbreviations 7

    Italics 8

    Word Division 8

3 Punctuation 9

    Periods 10

    Question Mark 10

    Exclamation Point 10

    Dash 10

    Hyphen 11

    Apostrophe 11

    Comma 12

    Restrictive Versus Nonrestrictive Elements 13

    Semicolon 15

Colon 15

Quotation Marks 16

Parentheses...17

Brackets..17

4 Spelling...**19**

Activity-1 19

Spelling Rules 26

5 Basic Sentence Structure **29**

Sentence Structure 29

Parts of a Sentence 30

Nouns..31

Verbs...32

Adjectives..34

Adverbs 35

Conjunctions and Prepositions 35

Preposition 36

Interjection 36

Sentence Problems 36

Sentence Variety..38

Steps for Proofreading...38

6 Active Listening and Interpersonal Communication Skills **39**

Listening Questionnaire..46

References 49

7 Improving Your Interviewing Skills...................................**51**

Witness Testimony...52

Hiring and Promotion...53

Closed-Ended, Open-Ended, and Probing Questions...................54

8 Report Writing **59**

What Is a Report? 60

Six Reasons for a Well-Written Report 60

Seven Essential Elements 61

Five Requirements of a Report..62

Fact Versus Opinion...63

Report #1 Investigation Report of Cell Fire.............................64

Report #2 Investigation Report of Cell Fire.............................64

Observation..65

Note-taking 66

Evidence 67

Log Entries 67

Bad Habits to Avoid...67

Activity 1: Observation 71

Activity 2: Observation 73

Activity 3: Observation 74

Reference...74

9 Common Reports Written by Criminal Justice Professionals.......... 75

Log/Activity Sheets/Chronologicals.......................................75

Presentence Investigations 76

Major and Minor Misconducts 78

Critical Incidents 79

Law Enforcement Arrest Reports 80

Use of Force 81

References 82

CHAPTER 1

A Professional Attitude

When we meet a person for the first time, it does not take long to form an opinion about that person. This opinion is based on several points including the persons' overall physical appearance, the manner of dress, and finally how the person speaks. Whether we like it or not, we are often judged by the way we use our language. Professionals, whatever the position or occupation, are expected to speak and behave in a professional manner. This, of course, is not easy or always achieved in our daily communication with others. However, there is really no excuse not to be able to write memos, correspondence, e-mails, and especially reports in a clear, concise, accurate, and professional manner. How do you, in your position, work toward and achieve what is called "a professional attitude" in your everyday work?

Allen and Bosta (1981) stated that professionals emulate several characteristics. They stated that professionals are capable of

- Believing in themselves and exuding self-confidence without the slightest hint of brusqueness or conceit
- Being reliable and emotionally stable, able to accept responsibility, and take independent action
- Controlling their situation instead of their situation controlling them
- Being firm but fair, which means adherence to the rules in a patient, constructive, and creative manner
- Displaying good manners and speech
- Being unselfish and not touchy
- Searching for truth instead of spreading rumors or gossip
- Not keeping account of evil or gloating over the wickedness of others
- Being neat in appearance and developing a friendly personality without becoming overly familiar
- Analyzing their speech and actions as well as the speech and actions of others

- Being humble, sympathetic, and understanding without divulging their own personal affairs or problems, or without allowing themselves to be distracted or given to favoritism
- Adapting to change, maintaining enthusiasm, dispelling prejudice, and showing allegiance to their employers
- Being alert, quick to respond, able to make decisions accurately and fairly, and concerned with the welfare of both staff and inmates (pp. 23–24)

Thus, a professional attitude is a state of mind. Most of us attempt to be professional in our appearance and behavior. In other words, we dress and act appropriately for the occasion, whether it is for work or leisure. We may have colleagues who do not take this same pride in their personal appearance and behavior, and the odds are they also have negative attitudes about other aspects of their job and lives. Attitudes toward your work and yourself start with you. If you are convinced something is important enough to do well, you will probably work toward doing your very best. Part of developing a professional attitude is convincing yourself there is a reason to respond in a particular way. Most of us tend to adopt behavior patterns closely allied to those around us, both in the workplace or while pursuing our leisure activities. This is okay unless those with whom we associate with exhibit deviant behavior. An extreme example of this would be Correctional officers imitating the behavior of criminals. Another example is the tendency for many of us to follow patterns of behavior learned from our parents and friends. We also behave much the same as our colleagues in our work situation. If the people around you treat you in a professional manner, that is, with trust and respect, you will probably react in a similar fashion. Unfortunately, it is not always that simple.

Criminal Justice personnel operate in a unique work situation. The hazards of the job are fairly obvious to anyone who has spent any time working with deviant populations. What is not as obvious to the casual observer is how easy it is to fall into the speech patterns of those you are surrounded by, namely, the deviants. You may get away with this if you are able to separate what you have to write from your oral speech, but that is not always easy to do. Ideally, staff should be able to remain calm in verbal confrontations and not resort to obscene or vulgar language even though he or she may be on the receiving end of such. Obviously, it is easy to say, but difficult to do. Again, a professional attitude and a willingness to try to use language without falling to the level of some of those individuals with whom you have to interact, which may take a great effort on your part. The professionalism resulting should be worth the effort. This is especially true of any written material you are responsible for whether it is a brief memo or a full-scale major incident report.

Although not mentioned by Allen and Bosta (1981), written communication is just as important as oral communication. Chapters 2, 3, 4, and 5 will give you the opportunity to *review* some basic writing skills that most of you have seen sometime during your schooling. It will be an easy review for some of you, but may offer a small challenge to those of you who missed some of this material the first time around. Remember, people will judge you whether they are supervisors at work or members of the general public by both what you write and how you write.

We cannot complete this chapter on developing a professional attitude without spending some time discussing the need for standards for all positions within the field of criminal justice. The very nature of our work requires a strong feeling of group cohesion among the workers. Soldiers who see action in war learn very quickly who they are able to depend on when the situation becomes dangerous. In a very real sense Corrections/Field Services and Law Enforcement Officers face similar peril every day they go to work. There is no room for inconsistency or lack of honesty among them. Officers depend on each other in life-threatening situations and when they give their word, there can be no question of credibility. Mutual respect between officers will only be achieved through high standards that officers demand of themselves, as well as those required by the department. High standards may be encouraged and maintained by several means. One rather obvious way is one that you are involved in right now—education. Requiring personnel to obtain more education will help ensure better performance by them in the future. The requirement of higher education standards also serves as a screening process. Those who are unwilling to pursue and complete the educational requirements will not be hired or advance in rank. This, of course, has not always been the case in the past. Today, though, our society often equates professionalism and standards with the education required of practitioners in a particular field.

In many states, the standards for Law enforcement are measured against the state police force. Without exception, those states with state police departments worth emulating have high educational standards, high personal appearance standards, and a positive attitude toward professional behavior and development.

Professionalism begins with you. If you wish to be treated in a professional manner, it will be necessary for you to set high standards for yourself and your fellow workers. Whether it is your personal appearance, your honesty and credibility, or your desire to improve your skills, all are important and start with your desire to develop a professional attitude toward your work.

Professionalism does not occur overnight, nor will it be observed in all of your colleagues. This condition should not be considered a reason for you not to maintain a professional presence. Your pride in your job and personal appearance will soon be obvious to those with whom you work. As higher standards are required and spread throughout criminal justice, the system itself will also improve. Always remember, a professional attitude toward your job starts with you!

Reference

Allen, B., & Bosta, D. (1981). *Games criminals play*. Sacramento, CA: Rae John Publishers.

The Mechanics of Writing

Before beginning any document, it is important to know the basic mechanics of writing. Writing is a process. The more you are aware of the rules, the better you can communicate. Many people believe that they are "poor" writers or "poor" spellers. By practicing these skills, you become more proficient. That is, anyone can become a good writer, but the effort must be put toward learning how. So, let us begin with the basics.

Capital Letters

The capitalization of words helps to highlight them. In general, proper nouns are capitalized and common nouns are not capitalized. A proper noun is defined as the name of a particular person, place, or thing. Examples of a proper noun are Warden Taylor, Pennsylvania, Mississippi River, and the United States Congress. Common nouns are more general and may represent a number or type of persons, places, or things. Examples of common nouns are teacher, city, legislative body, and state. Some words, depending on how they are used, may be either a proper or a common noun. Here are some rules to help you clarify whether or not to capitalize a word.

Capitalize the first word of every sentence:

The food was not served on time.   **Inmate Jones was called to see the nurse.**

Capitalize the first word of a direct quotation:

Mr. Smith said, "I do not know."   **"We need a food count," Officer Jones said.**

Capitalize when the word "I" is used as a pronoun:

The officer and I left together.   **I told him to pick up our checks.**

Capitalize the names of officers when they are used as titles:

Captain Thomas gave a direct order.   **The prisoner spoke to the captain.**

Capitalize the titles of official groups or bodies:

Michigan Department of Corrections Mecosta County Aging Commission

Capitalize *titles* when they precede a name:

Lieutenant Mike Kasher   **Father John Stevens**

Capitalize the proper names of courts at all levels:

United States Supreme Court   **Erie County Court of Common Pleas**

Capitalize the days, months, and holidays, but not the seasons:

Valentine's Day	**April**	**Christmas**	**Thursday**
fall	**winter**	**spring**	**summer**

Capitalize all references to a deity:

Allah   **God**   **Jehovah**   **Buddha**   **Savior**   **Messiah**

Capitalize the four principal directions on a compass—north, south, east, and west—only when you refer to them as geographical regions.

John planned to retire in the South.   **Jones is from the east side of town.**

Capitalize the names of roads, streets, avenues, places, boulevards, parks, and so on:

Forest Lake   **Fifth Avenue**   **Hemlock Park**

Capitalize the titles of books, magazines, and newspapers:

Topics in Criminal Justice   **Sports Illustrated**   **The Detroit Free Press**

Capitalize proper adjectives:

English   **Italian**   **Irish Spanish**

Writing Numbers

When to spell out numbers and when to keep them in tabular form may be confusing to the writer. While there is some variation in usage among publishers, the following rules are generally accepted. Be consistent in your writing. Do not use words for some and numerals for others in the same document.

All numbers ten and below should be spelled out.

There were only two arrests all day.   **There are four sergeants on duty.**

When comparing two numbers, use numerals.

Blocks 2 and 11 were locked down.   **Only 9 officers from 2nd shift compared to 52 officers from 1st shift signed up for the voluntary training.**

Numbers used to begin sentences should be spelled out even though they would ordinarily be represented in numerals:

Two hundred dollars was found on the inmate.

Twenty parolees are waiting for their parole officer.

Numerals should be used for street numbers, decimals, percentages, page numbers, measurements, and hours followed by A.M. or P.M.:

405 Fifth Avenue   **The metal was .42 inch thick.**

Prices were raised by 12 percent.   **He quoted from Chapter 8, page 30.**

Visiting hours were over at 9:00 P.M.

Use numerals after a dollar sign ($):

He received $50.80 for his work.

Use a combination of *words and figures for very large numbers*:

The state budget allowed $3.8 million for the project.

Use numerals when a number represents a specific place in a series, parts of books, tables, and so on.

Table 3 shows "Use of Force" incidents.   **Look at Chapter 4 for instructions.**

Abbreviations

In ordinary writing, abbreviations should be avoided or used sparingly. Abbreviations may be used in taking notes, but should not be used in final reports as they could possibly cause confusion or lack of clarity. The following are abbreviations that are considered appropriate in formal or informal writing:

Titles before proper nouns should be abbreviated only when the surname is given:

The prison hired <u>Dr.</u> Lambert. The prison hired a new doctor (not Dr.).

Months are only abbreviated when a date is used:

Feb. 18   (Jan., Mar., Apr., May, Jun., Jul., Aug., Sept., Oct., Nov., Dec.)

When in doubt about an abbreviation, use it only if you can find it in a dictionary.

Latin abbreviations such **as** <u>i.e.</u> (that is), <u>e.g.</u> (for example), and <u>etc.</u> (and so forth) are used quite often in most writing. Etc. is only used when the idea or ideas can be extended or continued.

Be prepared for class by bringing pencils, erasers, paper, etc.

In formal writing, such as reports, it is appropriate to write out titles unless they precede a proper name.

Sgt. Craig was late with her report.

The sergeant was late with her report. *NOT* **The Sgt. was late with her report.**

This is also true for nouns of countries, states, months, and days of the week.
On a Monday in **March, Ohio** changed its laws on drunk driving.

NOT

On a Mon. **in Mar., OH** changed its laws on drunk driving.

Italics

Certain words should be *italicized*. If a report is handwritten, underline what should be italicized.

Titles of books, journals, and magazines:	*Prison Journal*
Titles of plays, operas, motion pictures:	*Rent, Titanic*
Names of ships, trains, and aircraft:	*F22*
Names of newspapers:	*The Pioneer*
Names of legal cases:	*Estelle v. Gamble*

Foreign words and phrases that have not been absorbed in the English language should be italicized. It is best, though, to avoid phrases that are not easily understood. When in doubt, consult your dictionary.

Mi casa es su casa. (My home is your home.)

Italicize or underline words for special emphasis, but do not <u>overdo</u> it or you will be ineffective.

Word Division

The problem of where to divide a word is usually not an issue with word processing, but when handwriting reports or when using a typewriter, it is essential that certain rules of syllabication should be followed:

Do not divide words with one syllable and do not divide a word so that a single letter stands alone on a line.

weary not **wear-y**   **away** not **a-way**

When you have a compound word that already contains a hyphen, make the break where the hyphen occurs.

Well-informed *NOT* **well- in-formed**

Although most students have already learned these basic mechanics, it is good to refresh yourself with the rules. The next exercise provides the opportunity to check your weak areas.

CHAPTER 3

Punctuation

To write in a clear, correct, and effective manner, it is necessary to use proper punctuation. When expressing thoughts and how they are related to each other, we must show when to pause, when to stop, when to emphasize, when something will follow, and when something is more or less important. When speaking, we are able to indicate emphasis, enthusiasm, or a dramatic pause for effect. In writing, punctuation is used to accomplish this.

Punctuation rules are becoming more formal. Editors are using fewer punctuation marks today, partly because there is a tendency to use shorter and more concise sentences with less need for punctuation to clarify longer, more complex statements.

Professional writers, editors, and journalists generally set the standard for correct punctuation. You should remember that overuse of marks of punctuation should also be avoided.

The most important marks of punctuation are the following:

Period	.	Comma	,
Question mark	?	Semicolon	;
Exclamation point	!	Colon	:
Dash	—	Double quotation marks	" "
Hyphen	–	Single quotation marks	' '
Apostrophe	'	Parentheses	( )

The following are general rules to help make your writing clearer. The first type is referred to as "end" punctuation, which is essential to prevent confusion of ideas. End punctuation includes periods, question marks, and exclamation points.

Periods

The period is used to end a declarative sentence or an assertion or command:

The warden gave a direct order.   Close the cell door.

Use a period after most abbreviations.

Sgt.   Mrs.   Dr.   R.N.   C.P.A.   St.   M.D.   Ph.D.   Lt.

Periods should not be used after abbreviations for well-known organizations. When in doubt, check your dictionary.

FBI   ATF   UN   DEA   YMCA

Three periods together (...) are called *ellipses* and are used when you intentionally omit one or more words within or at the end of a sentence.

He hesitated ... spoke slowly and then quit speaking.

Use a period before a decimal, to separate dollars and cents, and to precede cents written alone.

.08 of an inch   4.3 percent $8.22 $0.35

Periods should appear after each number or letter symbol in an outline.

  I. **Officer Responsibilities**
   A. **Security of Institution**
   B. **Safety of Staff and Inmates**

Question Mark

Use a question mark when you ask a direct question or make a statement of doubt. Direct questions often begin with the following words:

Who?   What?   Where?   When?   Why?   How?   Action Taken?

When will visiting hours be over?   Where is the pre-sentence investigation?

If a polite request is phrased as a direct question, end it with a period.

Will you please inform me of the results.

Exclamation Point

An exclamation point is used to end a forceful interjection or to indicate surprise or great emotion.

Call the warden now!   Halt!

Dash

The dash is only used to indicate a sudden break or shift in thought.
   The em dash is a longer line and is used in place of commas, parentheses, or colons to enhance readability and emphasis of a phrase.

When I worked in Corrections - but you have already heard about that.

When the Correctional officers found contraband (all 20 cells in C Block), the warden ordered a complete shackdown of the prison.

OR

When the Correctional officers found contraband—all 20 cells in C block—the warden ordered a complete shakedown of the prison.

Use a dash to set off or to indicate strongly worded material.

The en dash is slightly smaller than the em dash and is used to represent a range of numbers, dates, time, or to separate two words that are connected, opposite, or indicate direction.

If you do well on your test-and work hard at your job- promotions will come.

Community corrections just published their new client handbook for 2019–2020.

Breakfast is served between 6:00 a.m. and 7:00 a.m.

Hyphen

The primary function of a hyphen is used for word division or the formation of certain compound terms.

The video on contraband was an eye-opener for staff.

Is there a money-back guarantee on these waterproof boots?

Apostrophe

The apostrophe has three general uses: (a) to show ownership, (b) to indicate omission of letters in contractions, and (c) to indicate the plurals of letters, some words, numerals, and symbols. In formal writing, such as reports, contractions should not be used, except when quoting directly.

The inmate did not follow my direct order.

The inmate said, "Don't touch my stuff!"

When a noun (name of a person, place, or thing) does not form its plural by ending in "s," add an **'s** to show ownership.

women – women's   child – children's

When the noun forms its plural by ending in "s," simply add an apostrophe.

guards' uniforms – more than one guard

cooks' recipe – more than one cook

When a noun has two "s" sounds in it, show ownership by adding an apostrophe alone. When the noun only has one "s" sound, add an "'s."

Officer Moses' handcuffs Kris's computer

When you have a compound noun, add the apostrophe and "s" to the last part of the expression, the one nearest to the object possessed.

father-in-law's car (singular possessive)

brothers-in-law's cars (plural possessive)

When you wish to show two or more people own something, make only the last noun possessive; for individual possession both nouns must have an apostrophe.

Blaze and Ben's Ipad (joint possession)

Shane's and Kaitlyn's laptops (individual possession)

When you form a contraction, it is necessary to use an apostrophe:

was not *becomes* **wasn't**   **does not** *becomes* **doesn't**

should not *becomes* **shouldn't**   **cannot** *becomes* **can't**

When you wish to form plurals of letters, numbers, and words, use an apostrophe and an "s."

r's   9's   two's

Remember, personal pronouns are already possessive by their very form and do not require the apostrophe.

His   hers   its   ours   yours   theirs   whose

Comma

The most widely used, and thus often misused, punctuation mark is the comma. There are few basic purposes for the use of a comma within sentences: (a) to introduce, (b) to separate, (c) to enclose, and (c) to show omission.

When you use an introductory word, phrase, and sometimes a clause, you follow it with a comma.

She had a decision to make, whether or not to file a grievance.

When the inmate moved toward me, I reached for the alarm.

When you introduce a short quotation, use a comma.

The officer replied, "See to it now!"

When you introduce a statement or question that is preceded by a mental question or thinking out loud, use a comma.

She thought to herself, what is this inmate up to?

I wondered, should I report this incident?

When you have independent clauses joined by conjunctions (as, and, but, neither, nor, or, yet), use a comma to separate them.

He did not like probation work, and his attitude reflected it.

It is the largest prison, but has the lowest critical incident rate.

When you have words, phrases, and clauses in a series, use a comma to separate them.

She locked the gate, turned in her report, and left for home.

The old prison cells looked out on narrow, dimly-lit corridors.

When you have two or more adjectives that equally modify the same noun, use a comma to separate them.

His clothing consisted of an old, dirty pair of pants and a new, expensive shirt.

When writing large figures, use a comma or commas to separate them.

The state prison population increased by 4,283.

When writing telephone numbers, house numbers, years, zip codes, serial numbers, license numbers, and decimals, commas are not used to divide the actual numbers.

The main complex has a new telephone number, 555-4328.

The new address is 525 Ferris Avenue, Tampa, Florida 33604.

The post was 28.47 inches high.

When enclosing parenthetical words, phrases, or clauses, use commas to enclose them. A parenthetical expression, which may be a word, phrase, or clause, may be omitted from a sentence without affecting the meaning.

The officer, however, was not prepared to give her report.

You are, on the other hand, better suited for corrections.

Restrictive Versus Nonrestrictive Elements

When restrictive and nonrestrictive elements are used in a sentence, it is necessary for the writer to determine how the specific phrase or clause contributes to the meaning of the word or words it represents. A *restrictive element* restricts or limits the meaning of the word or words it represents. Omitting a restrictive element would significantly change the meaning of a sentence. Restrictive elements are never set off with commas.

(Restrictive) **Corrections employees <u>who work hard</u> will advance in rank.**

A *nonrestrictive element* provides added information about the word or words it applies to, but it does not restrict or limit the word or words. A nonrestrictive element could be omitted from the sentence without changing the essential meaning. Nonrestrictive elements are always set off by commas.

(nonrestrictive) **The warden, <u>who graduated from Ferris State University</u>, received a bonus.**

If all of this is confusing to you, there is a test you can apply to determine whether an element in the sentence is restrictive or nonrestrictive. Does the meaning of the word that comes before the element change when the element is removed? If it does, then the element is restrictive. If it does not, then it is nonrestrictive. The sentence with the restrictive example "who work hard" definitely restricts "employees" who will advance in rank. In the sentence with the nonrestrictive example, "The warden" will still receive a substantial raise regardless of where he graduated from college and, thus, "who graduated from Ferris State University" is nonrestrictive.

When words are in apposition (words used to identify or explain a word or words they follow), they should be enclosed by commas.

John Webster, our warden, was on vacation. (Nonrestrictive)

Our warden, John Webster, was on vacation. (Nonrestrictive)

Warden John Webster was on vacation. (Restrictive)

When you use nouns, pronouns, or noun phrases in direct address, use commas to enclose them.

Dr. Barton, may I ask you to explain?   **May I ask you to explain, Dr. Barton?**

When you use initials or titles following a person's name, use a comma or commas to enclose or separate them from the name.

Eric Lambert, Ph.D., and Joe Smith, M.D. spoke to the Novi Training Council.

Michael Watson, Jr. lied to the investigator.

When you use places or dates that explain preceding places and dates, enclose with commas.

The prisoner left the laundry on March 9th, for his new work assignment.

Her new home is at 14 Fifth Street, Detroit, Michigan 48126.
(Note that you do not use a comma *before* or *after* a zip code number.)

When you use a comma that is unnecessary it is just as bad as when you omit a necessary one. Here are a few of the most common misuses of commas.
Do not use a comma before the first word of a series.

In the cell they found, a knife, a short pipe, and a rope.
(Comma after <u>found</u> is incorrect.)

Do not use a *comma* between two "independent" clauses where a semicolon or period is required. This misuse is called a comma splice and creates a run-on sentence.

The inmate told me to meet him, I told him I could not.
(Either a period, or semicolon should appear after <u>him</u>, not a comma).

Finally, do not use a comma unless you have a reason to do so. The comma is the most frequently used and the most important of all marks of punctuation. It will improve the clarity of your writing if used properly.

Semicolon

The semicolon is a stronger mark of punctuation than the comma, but not as strong as other terminal marks such as the period. It indicates a longer pause between sentence elements in comparison to the comma. The semicolon indicates that one idea has stopped, but a similar one will begin.

When you separate independent clauses not joined by a simple conjunction, use a semicolon.

Young inmates have certain attitudes when they arrive at an institution; as they put more time in these attitudes change.

When you wish to separate a series of items that are long and complex or that already contain a comma, use a semicolon.

The union vote 121 in favor, 136 opposed to accepting the offer; 180 agreed for the negotiators to stay and 77 stated they wanted to stop negotiations.

When you have groups of words that expand a single thought, use a semicolon to separate them.

We knew the problem at the prison was obvious, that the institution was overcrowded; there weren't enough cells; there wasn't enough concern to change the situation.

Use a semicolon when you need to separate lists of words or phrases or clauses that would be unclear if you used only commas.

Attending the Sheriff's meeting were Timothy Eklin, Director, Department of Corrections; Michael Mendenhall, Corrections Officer, Metropolis Prison; and Lt. Gregory Vanderkooi, Warden, Newaygo Prison.

Colon

Think of the colon as a mark of expectation. It indicates that a statement, a long quotation, a series, an example or an explanation or an example, will follow immediately after the colon. The rule is simple, use a colon when you have an independent thought that can stand alone, but the information after the colon explains or specifies what has been said earlier.

There are many tasks before leaving work: turn in keys, turn over the roster, return equipment, and sign out.

When you have introductory words for a long quotation, use a colon to separate them.

The warden concluded her talk to the new officers in a serious vein: "Each officer depends on his or her fellow officer for moral and physical support in order to get the day-to-day job completed."

When you have the following situation, use a colon as a separating mark. The salutation in business letters is separated from the body of the letter by a colon:

Dear Mr. Robison: **To Whom It May Concern:**

In writing time, separate the hour and minute figures by a colon:

6:35 A.M.   **4:50 P.M.**

When writing acts and scenes of plays, or chapters and verses of the Bible, use a colon for separation:

Shakespeare's *Julius Caesar*, II: IV   **Mark 2:2-4**

Quotation Marks

Quotation marks, either double (**"..."**) or single (**'...'**) are marks of punctuation used to indicate that you are stating something that has been said or written by you or someone else.

Officer Queen said, "Do it now or I'll write a ticket!"

or

"Do it now, or I'll write a ticket!" said Officer Queen.

The report stated, "Fifty new officers will be needed for the facility."

or

"Fifty new officers will be needed for the facility," the report stated.

When it is necessary to use a question mark, exclamation mark, and dash when using quotation marks, you need to decide whether the mark applies to the quoted material or to the entire sentence and place the mark accordingly.

Captain Lewis yelled, "Where are those inmates going?" (Quote asks a question)

What does the statement in the prison newsletter mean by saying, "Guards are both underpaid and overpaid"? (Entire sentence asks the question)

When using slang or uncommon technical words, use quotation marks.

Inmate Amey was noted for his "bad mouth."

The store did not stock "flash drives" for the new computer.

When writing titles of articles, short stories, short poems, newspaper articles, or chapter headings, enclose them in quotation marks.

The teacher assigned Chapter 2, "Stress for Success," for class.

The *New York Time's* article, "Tomorrow's Prisons," offered some frightening statistics.

When you wish to emphasize a word or phrase, set it off with quotation marks. Be careful not to overdo this in your writing. It is better to select the best word or phrase rather than using quotation marks for emphasis.

When you need to enclose a quotation within a quotation, use single quotation marks. This may also be used when using quoted material from another source to ensure the reader knows it is the exact wording.

Greg said, "Steve just called me 'a punk' so I punched him."

Parentheses

Parentheses ( ) are used to enclose material that helps explain material in a sentence.

The inmate (the one involved in the fight) does not deserve a lower classification level.

Parentheses are also used to set off reference citations that appear in the text.

The book stated that the criminal justice system seems to do what is more convenient despite good intentions (Rothman, 1980).

Brackets

Brackets [ ] are generally used to show comments, corrections, or additions to quoted material.

The guest speaker in the auditorium declared, "I am very unhappy [it was obvious he was furious from his facial expression] with your conduct at this assembly."

CHAPTER 4

Spelling

Have you heard or used the expression, "I am just not a good speller." It may be true, but it does not really solve the problem or relieve you of the responsibility. When writing, especially in a situation where you are rushed or need to convey a written message quickly, errors can be made. Interestingly enough, most people usually have little trouble with difficult words because we need to look them up in a dictionary or rely on spellcheck. However, too many times it is assumed we know the "easy" words and miss them in proofreading our own writing. Unfortunately, the misspelling of common words is regarded by the general public and colleagues as a sign of a lack of education. Those who are responsible for writing reports that are read by a wide audience, will be judged on the professionalism of the report and this certainly includes spelling as well as clarity.

Since spelling is really a skill, it can be changed with minimum effort by developing a professional attitude toward your writing. If you believe spelling is not important, then there will be no improvement. The exercises presented on the following pages will give you the opportunity to improve. Remember, once you have learned to spell a word correctly, it is yours forever.

One way to begin to improve your spelling is to identify words that are troublesome to you. We generally know or use less than fifty thousand of these words. The key, then, is to identify those commonly used words that we have been misspelling and to consult our dictionary or an online source (dictionary.com) when we have the slightest doubt on any other word. Is this tedious work? You bet, but the results are well worth it.

Activity-1

As you read the following list of commonly misspelled words, pronounce each one, cover each one with a piece of paper, and then write the word in the space provided. After you have completed the exercise, make a list of those words that gave you trouble. You may wish to do this exercise in stages rather than all at once.

A	
Abduction	Abscond
Absolute	Accessory
Accidental	Accomplice
Acquaintance	Acquittal
Adjudicate	Administrator
Admission	Adultery
Adversary	Advocate
Affiant	Affidavit
Affirmative	Aftercare
Aggravate	Aggregate
Alias	Alibi
Allegation	Amphetamine
Anonymous	Antisocial
Appeal	Appellant
Apprehend	Arbitrator
Arraignment	Arrest
Arsenal	Arson
Assailant	Assassination
Assistance	Attempt
Attorney	Autopsy
B	
Ballistics	Bailiff
Bankruptcy	Barbiturates
Battery	Behavior modification
Beginning	Belligerent
Bench warrant	Biographical
Bludgeon	Bona fide
Bond	Breathalyzer
Bribery	Bureau
Burglary	
C	
Cadaver	Cannabis
Capacity	Chain of command
Career	Censure
Chain of custody	Chronic
Circumstantial	Citation

Classification	Clearance
Clemency	Cocaine
Codefendants	Coercive
Cognitive	Collateral
Collusion	Commitment
Community	Commute
Compelling	Compensation
Complaint	Comprehensive
Concurrent	Condemnation
Conditional	Confession
Confinement	Conjugal
Conspiracy	Consecutive
Consent	Consensus
Constable	Constitution
Conviction	Cooperate
Council	Counsel
Counterfeit	Custody
D	
Decriminalization	Defendant
Deinstitutionalization	Delegate
Delinquent	Delusion
Demeanor	Dementia
Demographic	Deprivation
Detainer	Detention
Determinate	Deterrence
Detoxification	Discretion
Discipline	Disclosure
Dismissal	Disposition
Dispute	Disqualification
Dissent	Diversion
E	
Ecstasy	Embarrass
Embezzlement	Encumber
Entrapment	Equality
Equity	Eviction
Evidence	Execute
Exonerate	Expiation

Expunge	Extenuating
Extradition	
F	
Familiarity	Fatigue
Fentanyl	Fictitious
Forcible	Foreseeable
Forfeiture	Forgery
Fornicate	Forty
Fraud	Fugitive
Furlough	
G	
Garnishment	Government
Gratuity	Grievance
Guarantee	
H	
Habeas Corpus	Habitual
Hearsay	Heroin
Homicide	Hyperactivity
Hypothesis	
I	
Identification	Illegal
Illegible	Illiterate
Immunity	Implicit
Impulsivity	Inadmissible
Incapacitation	Incarceration
Incompetent	Incriminate
Indeterminate	Indictment
Inebriate	Insufficient
Intensive	Intermediate
Intoxication	Invalidate
Involuntary	Isolation
J	
Jeopardy	Judiciary
Jurisdiction	Jurisprudence
Juror	Jury
Juvenile	
K	
Kneeling	Kidnap

L	
Larceny	Laser
Legalization	Legible
Legislation	Legitimate
Lewdness	Libel
Lieutenant	Litigation
Loitering	Loose
M	
Magistrate	Maim
Malice	Malicious
Mandatory	Maneuver
Manipulation	Manslaughter
Marginal	Marijuana
Maximum	Mediation
Methamphetamine	Methadone
Milieu	Minimum
Miscellaneous	Misdemeanor
Mistrial	Mitigating
Monitor	Monogamous
Moot	Municipal
Mute	Mutual
N	
Narcotics	Narcissistic
Necrophilia	Negligence
Negotiate	Noticeable
Nolo contendere	Non Omittas
Nuisance	Nystagmus
O	
Objection	Observation
Obstruction	Occurrence Offender
Offender Occasion	Official
Opium	Ordinance
Overcrowding	
P	
Paramour	Paranoid
Parole	Participant
Pathologist	Pedophile

Penal	Penitentiary
Persecute	Personal
Personnel	Personality
Petition	Peyote
Pharmacology	Plaintiff
Polygamy	Pornography
Positivist	Precedent
Predisposition	Prejudicial
Premeditation	Preponderance
Presumptive	Privatization
Probation	Prohibition
Prosecution	Prostitution
Psychiatric	Psychedelic
Psychoanalysis	Psychology
Psychopath	Punitive
Purge	Pyromaniac
Q	
Qualified immunity	
R	
Ransom	Rational
Reasonable	Rebuttal
Recidivism	Recognizance
Reconviction	Recoupment
Referral	Reformatory
Rehabilitation	Reintegration
Reprieve	Residential
Respondent	Restorative
Retribution	Revocation
S	
Sabotage	Sadomasochism
Schizophrenia	Seizure
Segregation	Sergeant
Severance	Sexual harassment
Sheriff	Situation
Slander	Socioeconomic
Sodomy	Solicitation
Stability	Statute

Stereotype	Stigmatization
Stressors	Subjective
Subpoena	Sub-rosa
Substantial	Substantive
Summary	Suppression
Surety	Suspicion
Sustain	Systemic
T	
Tangible	Technical
Terrorism	Testimony
Therapeutic	Thorough
Through	Tier
Traditional	Transitional
Trespass	Typology
U	
Unconditional	Unconstitutional
Underclass	Urban
V	
Vacate	Vagrancy
Vandalism	Vehicle
Vengeance	Venire
Venue	Verdict
Victimization	Vigilante
Violation	Vocational
Voluntary	Voyeurism
W	
Waiver	Wanton
Warrant	Wiretapping
Witness	Wound
Y	
Yield	Youthful Offender
Z	
Zealous	Zero tolerance
Zigzag	Zoning

Hopefully, you have now been able to identify words that you need to be aware of in your writing. Remember, very few people are perfect spellers. Most of us must be alert whether we misspell words quite often or only occasionally. All of us can improve if we set this as a goal. Remember, an incorrect word may change the entire meaning of a sentence or paragraph. Criminal Justice personnel have a professional obligation to make their writing of memos, e-mails, and reports as concise and accurate as possible, not only because it is a vital part of their jobs, but it also reflects on their personal competence.

Here are a few ideas to help improve spelling and the use of words. These suggestions are painless, but do require a willingness to incorporate them into our daily routine.

1. Always proofread your writing. Sometimes it helps to read your work aloud. You may wish to have a friend read your work. If you are really a poor speller, it sometimes helps to read your writing backwards. This requires you to look at each word out of context.

2. You started a list of words on commonly misspelled words and homonyms. Add to it every time you misspell or misuse a word in your writing. As you learn to spell problem words correctly, strike them from your list.

3. Many times only a letter or part of a word will be misspelled. Underline these particular letters or parts of the word and work on memorizing the correct letters or parts.

4. When you look at a word, divide it into parts. If you mispronounce the word, you will probably have a problem spelling it correctly. When in doubt of the pronunciation of a word, ask someone or consult your dictionary or online source.

Spelling Rules

There are some rules that will help avoid some of the more common spelling errors. Unfortunately, almost all of the rules have exceptions.

Learn the "*i-before-e*" rule. The following mnemonic device may be helpful:

Write i before e

Except after c

Or when sounding like a

As in <u>neighbor</u> and <u>weigh</u>.

Before reviewing some other spelling rules, we need to quickly look at some terms used in these rules:

Vowels are the letters a, e, i, o, u, and sometimes y.

Consonants include all the letters in the alphabet except vowels.

A **syllable** is a word or part of a word pronounced with a single uninterrupted sound of the voice:

part = one syllable   **single = two syllables—"sin" and "gle"**

A **prefix** is a group of letters that, when added to the front of a word form another word related in meaning to the original word.

Prefix: **<u>mis</u> + interpret = misinterpret**   Prefix: **un + natural = unnatural**

A **suffix** is a group of letters that when added to the end of a of a word form another word related in meaning to the original word.

accidental + (suffix) **ly** = **accidentally**   **success** + (suffix) **ful** = **successful**

In monosyllables and words accented on the final syllable, if they end in a consonant preceded by a single vowel, double the consonant before a suffix beginning with a vowel:

bat + ted = batted   **commit + ting = committing**

In words ending in a silent **e**, the **e** is dropped before a suffix beginning with a vowel, but is retained before a suffix beginning with a consonant:

arrange + ing = arranging   **arrange + ment = arrangement**

In words ending in **y** preceded by a consonant, the "**y**" is changed to an "**i**" before any suffix except one beginning with **i**:

happy + ness (y to i) = happiness   **hurry + ed (y to i) = hurried**

Words ending in **y** preceded by a vowel keep their form when a suffix is added:

donkey + s = donkeys   **employ + ed = employed**

However, there are some exceptions to this rule:

pay, paid;   **lay, laid;**   **say, said.**

The following are rules for forming **plurals**:

Most nouns (names of persons, places, things, or ideas) form the plural by adding **s**:

king + s = kings   **boy + s = boys**

Nouns ending in **s**, **sh**, **x**, or **y** add **es**:

church + es = churches   **kiss + es = kisses**

Plural of words ending in **o** - and nouns ending in **a** preceded by a vowel form the plural by adding **s**:

folio + s = folios.

Nouns ending in **o** preceded by a consonant add **s** or **es**. Most of these words merely add **s**. Exceptions (which add **es**) are

Echo hero   **no**   **potato**   **tomato**   **cargo**   **mosquito**

Irregular plurals—some words that come to us from an Anglo-Saxon tradition form the plural with an **en** ending:

Children   **men**   **women**

Others have an internal spelling change:

Goose to **geese**   **Mouse** to **mice**

Plural of foreign words—there are many words in English that were borrowed from foreign languages (particularly Latin) that form the plural according to the rules of their own native tongue:

Alumnus = alumni   **Alumna = Alumnae**

Plural of compound words—compound words generally form the plural by adding **s** or **es** to the more important word in the combined form:

Mother-in-law = mothers-in-law

If the component elements form a solid word without a hyphen, the suffix is added to the end of the word:

Cupful = cupfuls

Basic Sentence Structure

In Chapter 4, we have reviewed some of the basic elements that go into the writing of sentences: words, punctuation, and mechanics. Combining these elements correctly will provide adequate sentences, but not necessarily the most effective. If sentences are awkward or unclear, your primary purpose for writing them will be ineffective. Remember, good sentences that are well structured and contain the best choice of words are needed to build good paragraphs. Effective paragraphs lead to more effective reports. To avoid cumbersome and less than clear sentences, think about writing sentences that have unity, clearness, and complete thoughts. To do this, it is necessary to know what a sentence is and understand the grammar and structure in its construction. After understanding these elements, you will be well on your way to writing direct and clear sentences.

Let us start by looking at *four* basic sentence structures. The classification of a sentence is determined by the number of main or subordinate clauses it contains.

Sentence Structure

1. To locate the **subject** of a sentence you simply ask, "*Who is doing the action?*"
2. To locate the **verb** in a sentence, you ask the question, "*What action is being performed?*"

S = Subject   **V = Verb**

A **Simple Sentence** has a single main clause and states one main idea or a thought.

S   V   S   V
The man died.   **The bird flew away.**

The sentence is still classified as a simple sentence when either the subject or the verb or both are compounded.

```
        S      S    V                     S    V      V
The man and woman died.          The woman fought and died.
        S      S    V      V
The man and woman fought and died.
```

A **Compound Sentence** has two or more main clauses, generally connected by conjunctions (or, and, but) or by a semicolon (;).

```
        S    V      S    V              S    V    S    V
The inmate fled and the guard fired.    The inmate fled; the guard fired.
```

Compound sentences will add variety to your writing and will help avoid a choppy writing style resulting from too many simple sentences. Do not fall into the trap of becoming too wordy or constructing sentences that, although grammatically correct, are too long and confusing. Clarity should always be your goal.

A **Complex Sentence** has one main clause and one or more less important clauses. In other words, there is a main thought with one or more supporting thoughts. Complex sentences may be used to make ideas or thoughts clearer. Rather than using simple sentences, combine them for clarity into a complex sentence.

Simple Sentences: The accident occurred ten miles outside of town. The sheriff needed help.

Complex Sentence: Due to the accident that occurred ten miles outside of town, the sheriff needed help.

A **Compound–Complex Sentence** contains two or more main clauses and one or more subordinate clauses.

When the judge pronounced the sentence, the defendant cried while the courtroom cheered.

Parts of a Sentence

We also need to examine briefly what goes into the various parts of the sentences. Of course, we are referring to words. Words are classified according to their use within a sentence. These are called parts of speech and every word in our language may be identified by its function as one of the following:

Nouns	Adverbs
Pronouns	Conjunctions
Verbs	Prepositions
Adjectives	Interjections

Nouns

A **Noun** is the name of a *person*, *place*, *thing*, or *idea*. There are three types of nouns.

Common nouns refer to ordinary persons, places, things, or ideas.

Persons:	**teacher, inmate, father, judge, priest**
Animals:	**cat, chicken, horse, pig, dog**
Places:	**courtroom, cell, house, jail, player**
Things:	**ashtray, radio, desk, cigarette, ice**
Ideas:	**democracy, honesty, integrity, freedom**

Proper Nouns refer to <u>specific</u> *persons*, *places*, *things*, or *ideas*.

Person:	**Warden McMillan, Father Murray, Officer Patton**
Creatures:	**Rottweiler, Clydesdale**
Places:	**Detroit, New York City, Cell Block 8**
Things:	**Ford Expedition, Kleenex, Sony**
Ideas:	**Socialist, Democratic, Catholicism**

Pronouns are substitutes for nouns and are used to avoid repetition in sentences. Pronouns are used to *speak of persons*, *places*, or *things you cannot name*.

She was unknown to us, but he knew her.

Pronouns are also used to refer to proper nouns without repeating them.

Sheriff Kasher dashed from his car and then he chased the suspect.

Pronouns may be used to refer to people or things in general terms.

We are happy with the decision.

A **Personal Pronoun** is a direct substitute for a noun as a subject or object. When the personal pronoun is the *doer* of the action or thought, it is the *subject* of the sentence. The following should be used.

Singular subject:	I	you	he	she	it
Plural subject:	we	you	they		

> **I** went to the meeting—**singular**   **We** went to the meeting—**plural**
>
> **He** broke the rules—**singular**   **They** broke the rules—**plural**

When the **Personal Pronoun** is the *object* or *receiver* of an action or thought, the following should be used:

Singular subject:	me	you	him	her	it
Plural subject:	us	you	them		

Jameson threatened **me**.   Jameson threatened **us**.

Officer Crane told **her**.   Officer Crane told **them**.

Possessive Personal Pronouns indicate ownership or used as a possessive.

Singular ownership: my, mine   your, yours   his , her, hers, its

Plural ownership: our, ours   your, yours   their, theirs

My car was stolen.   The car is **mine**.

The uniform is **hers**.   The uniforms are **theirs**.

Verbs

A **Verb** *expresses action, a state of being, or a condition; it says or asserts something.* Without verbs it would be very difficult to communicate clearly. We already know that nouns may be singular or plural; the same is true of verbs. When we construct sentences, the subject (noun) and the predicate (verb) must be in agreement. Active verbs usually end in an "s" when they are in singular form. The following verbs would require singular subjects: fights, hits, sings, talks.

He **fights** the system.   Anne **sings** the blues well.

When your sentence's subject is a plural noun or pronoun, you use a plural verb, that is, a verb that does not end in "s."

We talk together a lot.   The **officers hit** the panic button.

An exception to the above occurs when we use a plural verb with the singular pronouns "I" and "you."

I sing well.   **You talk** too much.

There are two reasons why problems arise because of errors in agreement. First, the writer is unsure about the number (singular or plural) of the subject because of other words in the sentence, and second, a verb is used to agree not with the grammatical form of a subject, but with its meaning. The writer must be able to identify the real subject and whether it is singular or plural. Let us examine some of these problems in more detail.

When you have two or more singular subjects connected by **and**, the subject is considered plural and requires a plural predicate verb.

Henderson, Smith, and I **ride** together to work.

If you connect singular subjects together by **or**, **nor**, or **but**, a singular verb should be used.

Neither Henderson **nor** Swanson **rides** together to work.

If you have a singular and plural subject joined by **or**, **nor**, or **but**, the verb must agree with the nearest subject.

Neither the warden nor the **counselors want** a confrontation.

Neither the counselors nor the **warden wants** a confrontation.

Certain pronouns, when used as the subject of a sentence, require a singular verb.

anybody	**everybody**	**no one**
anyone	**everyone**	**somebody**
each	**neither**	**someone**
either	**nobody**	

Everyone of the inmates is guilty of the attack.

Each of us needs to become more active.

When a title of a book, newspaper, magazine, journal, movie, play, or song is a subject of a sentence, use a singular verb even though the title may end in "s."

The Untouchables **is** a popular movie.

The Detroit Free Press **influences** thousands of people each day.

A **Collective Noun** takes a singular verb when it is considered as a unit, and a plural verb when the individuals represented by the collective noun are regarded separately.

The group has requested less work.	**The group have requested less work.**
(The group as a unit made the request.)	(Each one in the group made a request.)

When the word **there** is followed by a verb, it is singular or plural according to the number of subjects that follows. A singular verb should always be used after the word **it**.

There are strong arguments to release him soon.

In the center of the prison yard there stands a guard tower.

It is the inmates who must clean the cells.

A verb has three principal parts: **present tense**, **past tense,** and **past participle**. Most *regular* English verbs form their past tense and past participle by adding **d, ed,** or **t** to the present tense: jump, jumped, jumped; sleep, slept, slept. *Irregular* verbs form their past tense and past participle by a vowel change or an addition of an ending. Notice how these parts are used in the following sentences and then try the more confusing forms from the list of problem verbs.

I lift today.	**I lifted yesterday.**	**I have lifted every day this week.**
I speak now.	**I spoke yesterday.**	**I have spoken to him in the past.**

Sometimes we read our sentences carelessly and omit the proper ending of a regular verb.

Yesterday he asked (not ask) for permission to see his wife.

Verbs are also classified as to **voice**, either *active or passive*. When we use the active voice, it usually adds vitality and strength to our writing. The passive voice should be used sparingly in your report writing.

A verb is in the **active** voice when the subject is the performer of the specific action in the sentence. When the subject is inactive, does nothing specific, and has something done to it, it is in the **passive** voice.

Active: **The inmate saw the guard across the yard.**

Passive: The guard across the yard was seen by the inmate.

Active: **Lopez laid the weapon on the table.**

Passive: The weapon was laid on the table by Lopez.

Adjectives

An **Adjective** is a word that describes a noun or pronoun by making the meaning more exact. Often adjectives will answer the question of quality and quantity about the noun or pronoun. Other examples include size, age, shape, color, origin, material, purpose, emotion, sound, taste, touch, smell, weight, speed, temperature, brightness, and time.

old car   **ten** dollars   **blue** shirt

Adjectives often indicate greater or smaller degrees of quantity or quality by a change in form through the adding of "or" and "est" or the use of adverb modifiers: more, most, less, least. The use of "er" compares two persons or things, while "est" compares three or more things.

One jail: **The small jail was closed.**

Two jails: **The smaller jail was closed.**

Three jails: The smallest jail was closed.

Here are a few examples of the three degrees of comparison:

Positive	Comparative	Superlative
Big	Bigger	Biggest
Large	Larger	Largest
Slow	Slower	Slowest
Wise	Wiser	Wisest

Some comparisons are irregular; when in doubt, check the dictionary.

Good	Better	Best
Bad	Worse	Worst
Little	Less	Least
Much	More	Most
Some	More	Most
Many	More	Most

Certain adjectives cannot be compared because their meaning is absolute: square, perpendicular, empty, perfect, round, and unique. Something is either square or it is not. It cannot be more or less square.

Adverbs

Adverbs answer the question *of how*, *when*, *where*, *how often*, and *how much an action is to take place*. Adverbs are used to modify verbs, adjectives, or other adverbs. Most words that end in "ly" are adverbs. Some exceptions are holy, fatherly, manly, and sickly, which are classified as adjectives.

> They argued **heatedly** over the issue.
> (Argued how? Heatedly is an adverb modifying the verb argued.)
>
> **The officers arrived late to the meeting.**
> (Arrived when? Late is an adverb modifying the verb arrived.)

Adjectives may become adverbs with the addition of "ly." Some examples are slowly, sadly, and silently. As usual, we have exceptions. Some of the more commonly used are

Again	Not	Too
Almost	Now	Not
Also	Quite	Very
Ever	Sometime	Later
Never	Soon	

Adverbs can be compared in much the same way as adjectives.

Slow	Slower	Slowest
Near	Nearer	Nearest

When adverbs retain the same form, it is necessary to use **less** and **least** or **more** and **most** to indicate comparison.

Quickly:	**Less** quickly	**Least** quickly
	More quickly	**Most** quickly

Finally, there are irregular adverb comparisons that we simply need to learn or remember to consult a dictionary if we have a doubt.

Far	Farther	Farthest
Little	Less	Least
Some	More	Most

Conjunctions and Prepositions

Conjunctions and **Prepositions** are used as the connecting words in sentence structure. A conjunction joins words, phrases, or clauses. Conjunctions show the relation between the sentence elements that they join. Coordinating conjunctions (and, but, or, nor/ neither, for, since, so, because, until, yet, while) join words, phrases, or clauses of equal rank.

Words joined: The mess hall served lunch **and** dinner.

Phrase joined: Write to the warden **and** to the parole board.

Clauses joined: Raise your hands **or** get in the cell.

Preposition

A **Preposition** links a noun or pronoun with some other word in the sentence and shows the spatial (space), temporal (time), or the logical relationship between the object and the other word. The preposition, along with its object, almost always modifies the word to which it is linked.

Inmate Washington walked to the infirmary.
(**to** links infirmary to the verb walked; **to** the infirmary modifies walked.)

The distance between the front gate and his cell is forty yards.
(**between** links **gate** to the noun **distance**; between the front gate modifies distance.)

Commonly used prepositions are above, among, at, before, beside, between, down, during, from, in, of, over, through, to, toward, under, up, and with. Be aware that some prepositions may also be used as adverbs. When used as adverbs they never have objects.

Adverb: He went over. **Preposition: He went over the wall.**

Interjection

Interjections are used to express emotions. Such words have no grammatical relation to other words in the sentence. Strong interjections are followed by an exclamation point, while mild interjections are followed by a comma.

Stop! You are under arrest.

Look out, he will charm you out of your money.

Sentence Problems

We have examined the parts of speech that go into the making of a sentence. We will now look at some exercises that will make us aware of some problems that occur in the actual construction of sentences.

A **sentence fragment** is a part of a sentence incorrectly written as a complete sentence. Often, the fragment belongs to the preceding sentence.

Sentence Fragments	Corrected Sentences
The inmates enjoyed the show. Which was very entertaining.	The inmates enjoyed the show, which was very entertaining.
She called the control center. After having been locked out of her car.	She called the control center after having been locked out of her car.
My new dark green jacket worn with darker green pants.	I wear my new dark green jacket with my darker green pants.

Run-On sentences are two or more sentences written as one. They can be corrected in one of three ways: first, divide into complete sentences; second, divide the two sentences with a semicolon; and three, combine the sentences with a coordinating conjunction.

Run-On Sentences	Corrected Sentences
We went to the union meeting, it was late.	We went to the union meeting. It was late. OR We went to the union meeting; it was late. OR We went to the union meeting because it was late.
I understand you have a policy about this, however, I do feel that I deserve a second change to comply with it.	I understand you have a policy about this. However, I do feel that I deserve a second chance to comply. OR I understand you have a policy about this; however, I do feel that I deserve a second chance to comply. OR Even though you have a policy about this, I do feel that I deserve a second chance to comply with it.

Shifts in Person must be avoided (I, we, you, our, one, etc.). Do not make unnecessary shifts. Be consistent.

Shifts in Person	Corrected
If **one** enjoys being physically fit, **you** should work out as often as **you** can.	If **you** enjoy being physically fit, **you** should work out as often as **you** can.
If **anyone** needs a ride to work, **they** should call me.	If **anyone** needs a ride to work, **he** or **she** should call me.

Shifts in Tense must also be avoided. The tense of your verbs within the sentence must remain consistent. Shifts will confuse your reader.

Shifts in Tense	Corrected
It **was** a beautiful day, so we **are** going to permit the inmates more time in the yard.	It **is** a beautiful day so we **are** going to permit the inmates more time in the yard.

Shifts in Tense	Corrected
I **did** not understand what the warden **wants**.	I **did** not understand what the warden **wanted**. OR I **do** not understand what the warden **wants**.

Sentence Variety

Sentence variety is important to help keep your writing lively. One way to keep your writing interesting is to vary the length of the sentences. Too many short sentences in a row will create a choppy effect, while too many long sentences may lead to confusion. Try starting sentences with prepositional phrases. Use the active voice and include direct quotes when appropriate.

Steps for Proofreading

Writing clear and concise sentences takes practice. It is always a good idea to read, if possible orally, anything you write before sending it forward to be read by others. Proofreading is tedious work, but will pay dividends in the end.

It has often been said that the "Three R's" of writing are *revise*, *reword*, and *rewrite*. Whether you are writing an interoffice memo, a business letter, a letter to a friend, a set of instructions, or a major report, you should *always* go over the first draft looking for errors.

Here are some suggested steps to ensure that your writing is correct. **First**, read your draft out loud. This slows down your thought process and many times you can catch those minor errors. **Second**, pay attention to the tone of the language. Ask yourself if it is suitable for those who will be reading your writing. You may need to add more information or reword the material. **Third**, look for careless errors in grammar and sentence structure to ensure that your writing is not misinterpreted by the reader. **Finally**, try to select the best usage of words. Do not repeat major words unless you are doing so for emphasis.

Overall, your writing accuracy is a reflection of you. Proofreading to clean up mistakes and vague language is a must. This is not only true of reports, but also any electronic communication (such as e-mails or texts). Do not rely on automatic spell-checks as many times they substitute unrelated words. Bottom line, professionals proofread everything before they pass it on to the next person!

CHAPTER 6

Active Listening and Interpersonal Communication Skills

Criminal Justice personnel must have excellent interpersonal communication skills. These skills must constantly be worked on to provide the optimum level of effectiveness. Some people have a natural ability to get along well with almost everyone they meet. An immediate reaction to this statement might be, "But they have never worked with our clients!" This is a valid point. Communication does not occur in a vacuum. We are constantly being affected by all the signals and information from our environment whether it is at a social gathering or a cellblock. Most of us are able to develop, improve, or even learn skills that help us get along better with those we work with and those we associate with in our personal and social lives. Yet, there must be a desire to do so.

Well-developed interpersonal communication skills will not only make you more effective in your work, they will help make you a happier person. You become more successful on the job because you learn to resolve problems efficiently, learn how to say no when you should, and present yourself better by being able to express your feelings and ideas. Your personal happiness increases when you get along with colleagues and clients, and because you feel confident about working with others, you will have more self-respect. You also gain an appreciation for skills and personal qualities of those for whom you work; this, in turn, will increase respect from others as they begin to appreciate your directness and openness.

To achieve success in interpersonal communication, you need to understand what the term means. A simple definition of interpersonal communication is "Communication between people." We all communicate in our daily lives. We give simple directions, explain situations, and express feelings to friends and associates. What, exactly, goes on when we communicate? We have to use words to describe nonverbal experiences. All five senses are involved and sometimes it becomes very difficult to convey accurately our feelings or the situation to our own satisfaction. Therefore, communication is a process by which we organize, transmit, and interpret information picked up by our senses. It is, however, more than simply sending information from one source to another. Remember, we are concerned with effective interpersonal communication. What we have attempted to broadly define is communication. Interpersonal communication goes beyond this in that it is a uniquely human experience intended to send a specific message that takes into consideration the surrounding environment.

The objective of this chapter is to explain *effective* interpersonal communication. Effective interpersonal communication is something that can be different both in quality and achievement in every situation. We need to examine what it is that makes people effective interpersonal communicators. Effective interpersonal communication is not the simple process of a sender, a message, and a receiver, but rather a much more sophisticated approach, which is known as transactional. The *transactional approach* advocates the communication process as something we do <u>with</u> others rather than simply <u>to</u> others.

To be effective, we must be willing to adapt to the differences of those around us. We all vary in thoughts and experiences, which affect our beliefs, values, and attitudes. Many of our *beliefs* come from personal experience developed over a long period of time whereas values develop from our beliefs. Beliefs influence how we look at the world in general while our values determine how we behave in that world. *Values* result in standards of behavior. Many times the group, such as inmates, will determine the values. New members to a group quickly acquire the behavior pattern that is considered "right" or "wrong," "good" or "bad." We all tend to drop the values of an old group when we become members of a new organization or group. Sometimes, and this is certainly true in Corrections, we find we have conflicts when we feel we must maintain two different standards to be part of conflicting groups. Language may serve as a good example. Often Corrections officers will start to use coarse language similar to the inmates with whom they work; it is part of the group behavior. They, then find such language is not acceptable on the "outside," or that they are being judged by a different standard.

Attitudes, while similar to values in that we tend to behave according to them, are not as strong and as a result do not always affect our actual behavior. Attitudes can be changed easier than beliefs or values. We might have a "bad attitude" toward someone or an issue today, and then change tomorrow.

Most of us have been influenced by our past experiences and have developed into unique individuals who view ourselves, others, and our environment in a particular way. Sometimes, unfortunately, our perceptions are not always accurate. To be the most effective interpersonal communicator you can be, you must be willing to realize that there may be possible inaccuracies in your beliefs, values, and attitudes.

How do we do this? We need to learn to express ourselves. Let others know who you are and how you feel so they will know what to expect from you. If you are willing to do this, the odds are that you will get to know others because they will be willing to share information about themselves.

Think carefully before you speak. Try to be precise and be sure those to whom you are speaking understand what you are saying before continuing. Always try to present a confident, but not arrogant, attitude. Know the points you want to make, be pleasant, and speak clearly. Essential to all of this is your listener, whether it is a fellow staff member or a client. Keep in mind the listener's background, knowledge of your subject, personal feelings, and what your message will mean to him or her.

And now we come face-to-face with one of the most, if not the most, important communication skill—*listening*. To learn good listening skills, which most of us lack, is to improve your overall communication skills dramatically. Listening is not the same as hearing; it is understanding the meaning of another person's words, and more importantly, the ideas and feelings behind them. Depending on the study you wish to cite, we are told at least 40% of our daily communication is spent listening (Watkins, 2007). Radio, phone, television, lectures, sermons, and orders are a few examples of daily communication.

While the need to be a good listener may seem obvious, why do so many of us do it poorly? When we listen well we are able to accurately respond. This saves time, avoids confusion and mistakes, and will improve personal relationships. In the workplace, good listening can make us aware of what our supervisors expect of us and will enable us to be more effective in our interaction with those around us. In the case of Corrections officers, this would include both colleagues and inmates. When we listen well, we increase our range of friends and our family members will appreciate us even more.

As you approach specific ways of improving your listening skills, and thus your overall interpersonal communication, you need to examine some ideas about listening that many tend to believe, but are really false. Questions do not necessarily mean you are not listening, but could show you are interested and want to understand the speaker. Good listening means involvement. In school we are taught how to write, to speak, and to read, as well as other academic subjects, but seldom do you hear about a course being offered in listening.

It becomes obvious how important listening is and how often we misunderstand others and others misunderstand us. One misconception we need to eliminate from our thinking is that listening does not require any effort. Effective listening takes a conscious effort as it is really more difficult than talking. The good news is that we can all learn to be good listeners if we place this as a top priority in our lives.

There are a number of things that affect our ability to listen well. One of the most obvious may be termed external distractions. Noise, television, radios, telephones, excessive temperature changes, bright lights, and so on, can all reduce our concentration. If these distractions are present when you are giving or trying to obtain information, you need to do what you can to reduce the distractions such as moving to another area for the conversation or waiting until there is a more favorable time to exchange information.

Sometimes we simply are not as alert as we need to be. We may be tired or not feel well or the opposite, be too content and comfortable. In either situation, we may end up not concentrating and not listening well.

Another problem arises when we prejudge the speaker. All of us have prejudices; some of these are stronger than others. If we are aware of them, we can compensate and concentrate on the message. Sometimes we may be affected by the speaker's race, religion (if we are aware of it), sex, culture, appearance, accent, a very weak or very strong voice, or either poor or very eloquent delivery. Sometimes a speaker impresses us to the point that we do not really listen to the words. Some very successful politicians have been able to fashion careers on charisma alone because voters were not listening closely to what they were saying or they did not discern the lack of real meaning behind the words.

If we have a view on the idea being expressed, it is often difficult to remain patient and listen to the entire idea being expressed by the speaker. Related to this is the danger of not concentrating if the topic bores us, even though it may be important information.

It is not unusual for us to start to plan a response to a point the speaker is making, especially if we disagree with that particular point, and then not listen to all the information presented. Tied to this point is the danger of assuming we already know what the speaker plans to say. We may also decide the speaker is talking beyond our means to understand because of his or her vocabulary and we give up trying to understand the points being made. For example, a supervisor may ask for a report as soon as possible and be thinking of having it on his or her desk by the end of the working day. You may interpret the request that you have several days to complete the task. Also, when we bring problems to work with us or we have our minds on activities of the day, it is easy to become preoccupied and not listen to the speaker closely.

We mentioned that we have to guard against boredom if we wish to be good listeners. The mind may also become bored for brief periods of time because our minds are capable of processing what it hears at a much greater rate than most people speak. Estimates vary, but generally people speak at a rate between 125 and 200 words per minute while the rate of comprehension is between 400 and 600 words (Allee, 2007; Lamons, 1995). If a speaker has a slower delivery rate, you must concentrate to keep your mind from wandering.

There are several tips you may use to become an effective listener. The ideas we present here are simple enough, but you must be convinced that you need to employ them if you expect to become a more effective listener. When you really want to listen to someone, make sure the environment is conducive to listening. When you do not have control of the environment, such as in a noisy cellblock, at an athletic event, in the mess hall, or any number of other situations, you will need to make a special effort to hear as well as listen. If possible, when you are in control of a situation, such as a meeting, make every attempt to reduce distractions, such as noise, phone calls, glare from the sun on the speaker or the listeners, uncomfortable room temperature, or anything else that interferes with the ability to concentrate, and thus listen well.

You, as a listener, will be more effective if you try to be interested in the speaker. You may do this by making frequent eye contact . . . do not stare . . . but look at the speaker often and encourage the speaker with comments as "please continue" or "go on." It is not necessary to agree or disagree with the speaker's position at this time. That brings up another very important point. As we listen, we have extra time because our mind processes information more rapidly than most people speak. This extra time should be used to ask yourself a series of questions and this, in turn, forces you to listen well. What does the speaker mean? Will I learn something from this? Does this person know his or her topic? Are the points made sustained by the particular facts presented or have essential elements been left out?

There is a great temptation to break in on a speaker to correct, change the subject, or even provide words to help finish his or her thought. If you find yourself doing this, you probably are not a very good listener. There are times, though, when you should interrupt politely to ask a question to clarify something you do not understand.

All of these suggestions require you to be patient. We often form opinions before the speaker has completed his presentation or a point in a conversation. We all make mistakes at one time or another and we all should be given time to correct them whether in a formal presentation or in a one-to-one conversation.

Listeners in the classroom, at meetings, or when receiving work orders will often take notes. If you permit yourself to become too involved in the actual taking of notes, you may miss the essential points. Try to record only the main points, especially new facts and ideas. If you heard them before, the odds are you need not record them again. Try to look at the speaker frequently. In Chapter 8, more space will be devoted to the subject of effective note-taking.

Emotions are an important part of the listening process. When a person speaks to you, be aware of changes in the voice. We can determine by the pitch of the voice if stress is present or fast-paced delivery may indicate excitement. Slower responses may be a sign that the speaker is not sure of himself or herself or reluctant. A certain emphasis on words may show sarcasm or anger or exasperation by the speaker. As an effective listener, you must be aware of these differences. How loud a person speaks could signal anything from excitement to anger. Softness may show worry, secretiveness, or nervousness. Many of these interpretations are automatic by the listener. The problem is that we may misinterpret emotions and not "listen" to what is really being said. The listener must also recognize his or her own emotions and attempt to be objective in the listening situation. This, of course, is difficult to do in stressful situations that are common in criminal justice. Add to this verbal abuse in the form of obscenities, cursing and gestures, and Criminal Justice personnel are faced with a challenge to remain calm and sort out what is really being said in a specific situation.

When a person expresses certain feelings, we may wish to react by agreeing or disagreeing because of our own position or emotional relationship to the speaker's comments. Try to remain neutral and reflect back to the speaker and what he or she has said. By doing this you give yourself a chance to determine how accurate your interpretation is, and it presents the opportunity for the speaker to clear up any misunderstanding or misinterpretation on your part. When you are not sure of a person's comment, you may wish to ask a question for clarification.

If a speaker is conveying strong feelings to you, the initial reaction is often to want to give advice to help resolve the situation. While difficult for us to do, it is sometimes best to simply listen and give the speaker a chance to say whatever is bothering him or her. This talking out by speakers may produce enough confidence to have them seek answers on their own.

You must also learn to listen to or observe nonverbal clues. The voice may be saying one thing while the eyes and body of the speaker are conveying a completely different message. It is absolutely imperative that staff develop the skill to read body language. With practice, you will be able to observe signs of nervousness such as unnecessary movements with the hands, fidgeting, avoiding eye contact, tapping a foot, or any number of other actions. How a person sits or stands will provide you with clues relative to the speaker's confidence or lack thereof. A person who sits or stands with an alert look, good posture, and open stance will tend to exude confidence. The opposite is also generally true; eyes down, clenched fists, and arms held tightly to the side or across the chest may be indicators of defensiveness and a lack of openness.

Before you conclude that reading nonverbal clues is rather obvious and almost instinctive, it should be pointed out that most nonverbal signals may be open to more than one interpretation. Some people may stand or sit in a particular fashion because it is comfortable for them and for no other reason. To help ensure more accurate interpretation of body language, always try to look for two or three nonverbal clues as well as verbal indicators.

When listening to a speaker in a formal or informal setting and the presentation or conversation comes to an end, this is where you can improve your listening by translating the key points of the speaker into your own words. If there is a need to respond, try to identify areas of agreement before mentioning points of disagreement. Do you need for the speaker to elaborate further on what has been said? Now is the time to ask questions, especially open-ended ones that will require the speaker to expand on answers rather than a simple "yes" or "no."

Corrections staff will need to interrogate inmates at various times, but in normal conversation, staff should try to keep questions from sounding like an interrogation. If stress is involved on the part of the speaker, work to help him or her calm down. If a person is at ease, there is a better chance for accurate speaking and listening.

In our everyday lives, there are times when it is difficult to listen well. When we are too busy with work that needs to be completed or simply tired, we may not listen as well as we need to. Recognize these times and postpone important conversations to a time and place where you can devote your full attention. Many times we do not listen well to those closest to us such as our spouses and our children. When we are not able to devote our full attention, it may be better to postpone the conversation to a better time.

If you want people to listen to you, it is necessary that you speak clearly and express yourself simply and with concern for other's feelings. The odds are that if you are a good listener yourself, you will, in turn, be listened to.

Good listening will become a habit if you are willing to identify your barriers to good listening and avoid them, if you are willing to give the speaker your full attention, if you always try to fully understand the words being used and the ideas they represent, and if you are patient and willing to acknowledge the speaker's feelings without judgment until you have heard the entire message. Finally, if you are not sure what you have heard, ask questions.

It was mentioned earlier that most of us are poor listeners even though a large percentage of our workday is spent listening. Without training or a special effort on our part, it is estimated that we listen at only 25% efficiency (Lamons, 1995). Lamons gives two reasons for this. One is that we rather talk than listen. Second, since our brain processes the information faster than people can speak, we become bored. This is neither new information nor startling. Ralph Nichols (1957), known as the "father of listening," suggested 10 skills we need to develop to become good listeners. The 10 points are presented here as a summary of our discussion on improving your listening skills.

First, find an area of interest. Work at being interested in the topic under discussion. Poor listeners usually declare a subject dry after the first few sentences. We need to say to ourselves, "What is the speaker saying that I can use? What good ideas does he or she have? Is the speaker giving me some workable procedures? Are there any points I can use or will help me in some way?"

Second, we should judge content, not delivery. We excuse ourselves from listening carefully to a speaker by thinking, "Who could listen to this character? What a terrible voice!" or "Look at his appearance!" What we should ask ourselves is, "Does this speaker know some things that I need to know?"

Third, do not become upset or jump to conclusions that are not accurate after only listening to a speaker for a few minutes. Often a speaker will touch upon a pet peeve or belief in a way with which we disagree. We often want to argue with the speaker either orally or in our minds and thus do not always listen. We must be sure we thoroughly understand the speaker's point or position and withhold our evaluation until we do.

Fourth, a good listener will focus on the central idea or theme in a talk. A well-organized speaker will give cues to the listener. A poor listener will attempt to absorb too many facts too quickly and will miss the message. The old adage, "You cannot see the forest because of the trees" applies here. Learn to recognize transitions and organizational patterns.

Fifth, note-taking may be helpful if you do not overdo it. Most of us need help in remembering all the points we hear, but if we try to take too many notes on everything being said, we may miss the main theme or point of the talk. Take notes if you think it will help, but do not think you have to record everything.

Sixth, it takes real effort to listen well. We need to give each speaker our attention and indicate that we are listening by our facial expressions, our eye contact, and our posture. Feedback enables the speaker to be more expressive and as listeners, we will benefit as a result.

Seventh, as listeners we have to fight physical distractions to the listening process. The listening environment may be improved by merely closing a door to shut out noise, or opening a window to air out a stuffy room, or asking a speaker to speak louder. At times we may have to tolerate less than ideal situations in the work environment or even in a classroom on a hot, humid day. If conditions are not ideal and cannot be easily changed, then we must be willing to concentrate to get as much as possible from the speaker despite a bad situation.

Eighth, learn to listen to a variety of messages. We often turn off something that may be technical or outside our immediate area of expertise. Work at developing a desire to listen to different types of talks or presentations. We will develop and challenge our mental abilities if we are willing to try.

Ninth, we talked about physical blocks to good listening; we also have to be alert to psychological blocks. When the speaker touches upon a pet peeve, a particular conviction or value, and we are in disagreement, red flags go up and we resent the invading of these areas. Once we learn to identify our blind spots and learn to set them aside and hear the speaker out, we will develop into more effective listeners. The older the conviction, belief, value, pet peeve, or notion, the more difficult it may be for us to listen well.

Tenth, most of us are capable and actually do listen at the speed of about 500 words per minute while, as mentioned earlier, most of us speak at a rate of about 125 words per minute. What this means is that we have excess time to be distracted unless we do something about it. This may be even more of a problem if the speaker has a slow delivery rate. Effective listeners will make use of this excess time by constantly relating his or her own thoughts to the speaker's points. Studies indicate that this failure to utilize extra thinking time is one of the greatest problems facing the person who wishes to become a good listener.

The following inventory will enable you to assess your own listening skills. As you read the questions, try to determine how well you actually listen in the situations presented. The more accurate you are, the more valuable the results.

Listening Questionnaire

Respond to each of the following questions concerning your perceptions of your listening behavior. Print the appropriate number in the blank to the left; using the key below:

5 = almost always
4 = usually
3 = sometimes
2 = infrequently
1 = almost never

REMEMBER, all statements pertain to your listening behavior with superiors, subordinates, and colleagues in the work environment.

_____ 1. I weigh all evidence before making a decision.

_____ 2. I am sensitive to the speaker's feelings in communication situations.

_____ 3. I approach tasks creatively.

_____ 4. I concentrate on what the speaker is saying.

_____ 5. I use clear and appropriate words to express my ideas.

_____ 6. I encourage others to express their opinions.

_____ 7. I am able to see how different pieces of information or ideas relate to one another.

_____ 8. I listen to the entire message when someone speaks, whether I agree with what they have to say or not.

_____ 9. I let the speaker know immediately that he or she has been understood.

_____10. I remember what I am told even in stressful situations.

_____11. I recognize the main points when listening to an oral presentation.

_____12. I am sensitive to a speaker's vocal cues in communication situations.

_____13. I provide sufficient feedback to people when they are talking to me.

_____14. I consider the speaker's mood in understanding the message being presented.

_____15. I hear what is said when someone speaks to me.

_____16. I give an individual my complete attention when he or she is speaking to me.

_____17. I take into account situational factors that influence interactions when someone is speaking to me.

_____18. I can recall the specific information someone gives me several days later.

_____19. I respond in an appropriate and timely manner when someone is finished speaking to me.

_____20. I am ready to listen when approached by a speaker.

_____21. I notice the speaker's facial expressions, body posture, and other nonverbal behaviors.

_____22. I wait until all the information is presented before drawing any conclusions.

_____23. I allow for the fact that people and circumstances change over time.

_____24. I overcome distractions such as the conversation of others and background noises when someone is speaking to me.

_____25. I accurately understand what is said to me.

_____26. I seek information for better understanding a situation.

_____27. I communicate clearly and directly.

_____28. I focus on the main point of a message rather than reacting to details.

_____29. I am receptive to points of view, which differ from my own.

_____30. I time my communications appropriately, considering when to speak as well as what to say.

_____31. I remember the details of things that were said weeks or months ago.

_____32. I interrupt before a speaker is finished talking.

ADD YOUR ANSWERS AND COMPARE YOUR TOTAL BELOW:

128–160	SUPERIOR LISTENER
113–127	ABOVE AVERAGE LISTENER
80–112	AVERAGE LISTENER
65–79	BELOW AVERAGE LISTENER
32–64	POOR LISTENER

Your score is only as accurate as you were accurate in answering the questions. If you are curious, you may wish to have a close friend at work answer these questions about you and then compare both scores.

By now, it should be obvious to you that listening is one of the major components of interpersonal communication, but certainly there are others of similar importance. Listening carefully provides you the opportunity to respond in an intelligent fashion. This provides what is known as "feedback." Good feedback should contain three elements: (a) if you agree or disagree with points made by the speaker, be specific rather than general in your comments; (b) attempt a logical reaction rather than an emotional one; and (c) be tactful by trying to say something positive even if you disagree. You are more likely to reinforce a speaker with positive feedback than negative. However, negative feedback is necessary when you disagree with specific points made by a speaker. Such feedback will be more effective if you are ready to explain why you disagree and make it clear to the speaker that you are attacking the idea or point of view rather than the person presenting the information.

Being assertive is an important part of effective interpersonal communication. You need to be honest and direct with people while still showing respect and tactfulness. You have a right to disagree or say "no" when you have a good reason for not doing something. Nonassertive people are often taken advantage of and then become angry for permitting others to use them. Assertiveness, not aggressiveness, generally helps people to be happier in their work and also to be more efficient.

Interpersonal skills may be improved in several other ways. Both Probation and Correctional officers are placed in situations resulting in stress and must learn to recognize their own personal feelings. What physical reactions occur? How do you recognize these reactions when you are angry or upset with someone? Do you get an upset stomach? Do the palms of your hands become moist? Recognizing your personal reactions is only a beginning. Next, you need to question yourself as to whether these feelings are justified. Have you overreacted to a situation? Are your emotions causing you to react in an unfair way or preventing you from thinking clearly or logically about the situation or the person to whom you are listening?

When you learn to recognize the signals of your own body, you can begin to practice positive ways to deal with stress or anxiety during the communication process. Practice taking deep breaths; think carefully about what you are going to say; if appropriate, ask questions for clarification of possible misunderstandings. Always remember that nonverbal language will convey powerful messages, and a smile and friendly tone in your voice will convey as much or more than words alone. The opposite, of course, is also true.

There is little doubt that you will be faced with problems and conflicts on the job. These confrontations could be with other staff or with clients. We may be inclined to avoid conflict, but since it is probably impossible to do so we need to realize that it has some benefits. As a direct result of conflict or confrontations, people can get to understand themselves and those around them better. By examining both sides of an issue, there is a chance for making better decisions. Solving conflicts requires us to work together and this could result in better overall relationships. Working together to solve a problem, in itself, can be stimulating and rewarding if we know some of the techniques needed to resolve disagreement.

Techniques that will be useful to you are fairly obvious, but need to be in sequence to be the most effective. *First*, identify the problem, being as specific as you possibly can. Go after the issue. Forget past differences or disagreements. Be objective when stating the problem and tell how it developed. Do not blame people or a particular person for the problem, although there may be a great temptation to do so. Your purpose is to present the problem as clearly and concisely as possible.

The *next* step is to do a little "brainstorming" for solutions. With those present, generate as many solutions as possible. Some ideas offered may appear frivolous or impossible to act upon. Do not be critical. The more ideas offered, the more you have to choose from later on. It is easier to cut out than to add on, and it is helpful to have a host of ideas that you may be able to modify.

The *third* step is to list all the solutions offered and to evaluate them against the objectives or goals you have set. This is where you try to meet the needs of everyone present. Resources available, time, personnel, and policies are considerations that will help you evaluate the suggested solutions. Eliminating several of them will be fairly easy. Others may be more difficult. Probably any solution you decide upon will require some compromise on everyone's part. As long as everyone has been actively involved in the process, the chances are good that the solution will win support from those who worked to bring about resolution of the conflict.

Finally, once a solution has been decided upon, it is important not only to have a plan to get it started, but also to test the results. Establish some short-range goals and check to see if they are being accomplished. If they are not, you may need or wish to start the process over.

Effective interpersonal communication starts by you having confidence in yourself. You need to realize that you have something to offer and what you have to say is important and your ideas should be heard. We all need to be willing to share our ideas and points of view. When we meet with aggressive or hostile responses, we may defuse them by sticking to relevant issues and asking those involved to be more specific with their examples. Try to ignore emotionally generated responses. Realize that on some issues you may never agree, but that should not stand in the way of identifying areas of concern with which you do agree and continue working toward solving them.

Developing good listening and effective interpersonal skills requires a desire for self-improvement. Any effort in this direction will be rewarded by your becoming happier, respected, and more effective not only on the job, but in your everyday life. Be positive, share your ideas, and listen to others, and your interpersonal skills will improve each day.

References

Allee, S. (2007). *Speechwriting questions*. Retrieved from http://www.sheilaallee.com/questions.htm

Lamons, R. (1995). Good listeners are better communicators. *Marketing News*, 29 (19), 13–14.

Nichols, R. (1957). Listening is a 10 part skill. *Nation's Business*. 56–60.

Watkins, K. (2007). *How much time do you spend listening?* Retrieved from http://www.alumbo.com

CHAPTER 7

Improving Your Interviewing Skills

There are several reasons why you should want to improve your knowledge of interviewing techniques. The first reason is that you will be interviewing for a job and will want to make the best impression possible. You also may be interviewed several times by different people. Once you are employed, it will be necessary for you to undergo interviews when you seek to advance your position within an agency. Another reason for improving your interviewing skills is to make you more effective on the job. It will be necessary for you to conduct informal as well as formal interviews with clients, family members, and even witnesses. Your ability to conduct these interviews in an effective fashion will greatly enhance your usefulness. Finally, you may be interviewed as part of your job, such as when you witness an incident that results in criminal prosecution.

Reduced to very basic terms, an interview is an exchange of information. Usually this involves the interaction between two or more people. This exchange does have an extended meaning in that when two people interact the results are more than the sum of the two people involved. The interaction that occurs is an application of principles of interpersonal communication as well as the behaviors of those involved, which becomes an additional factor to be considered. Group interviews, sometimes called stress interviews or panel interviews, are becoming very common in criminal justice in the hiring and placement of new employees. These "Selection Interviews" will be discussed in detail later.

One other aspect of an interview is that at least one party has a reason, a distinct purpose, or a motive for the interaction. You should not assume that interviews are only conducted by professionals in formal settings. In a broader context, interviews are used in our daily interactions. The use of questions in an improper or poorly organized way may be just as much a hindrance to an informal interview situation as in a more formal job interview.

Always keep in mind that an interview is not a one-way process directed by one person toward another. If there is a failure to exchange information by any of those involved, a true interview has not occurred. An interview goes beyond casual conversation; *it has a purpose and is designed to achieve a goal.* Interviews may be used to obtain a position, obtain information about an incident, obtain information for evaluative purposes or counseling and, of course, you will be interviewed as a witness in investigations or legal proceedings when a crime has been committed that you have observed while working.

Messages are being exchanged between the interviewer and interviewee at the same time. Remember, nonverbal communication is an essential part of the interviewing process. A raised eyebrow, a shrug of the shoulders, crossed arms, or any number of other signals may indicate acceptance or rejection of an idea or question or it could present you with clues to an overall attitude about the interview. You, in turn, may be giving similar signals either consciously or unconsciously.

Witness Testimony

As mentioned earlier, you may be asked to testify as a witness to an incident you observed or were a part of during the performance of your job. As a witness, you will be asked to testify honestly and fairly to whatever you observed. Also, as a witness, you will be interviewed by law enforcement officers and lawyers. Being an effective witness is important not only for the obvious reason that justice may or may not result from being effective, but it also reflects on your ability. How well did you observe the incident? Did you make notes immediately? Were you objective and professional in your appraisal of this situation?

It is not unusual for people to be apprehensive about appearing in court. A brief review of the judicial process at this point may help alleviate some of the apprehension and make you a more effective witness. If you are needed to testify in a specific case, you will receive a subpoena (also called a summons), which is an official order from the court telling you where and when to appear at a trial or hearing, what you need to bring, and who to call if you need more information. Follow the directions exactly; the subpoena is a legal order, and to not follow it could result in a "contempt of court" charge by the judge.

When possible, try to visit the courthouse prior to your appearance to become familiar with the surroundings. This should help you gain confidence and be more comfortable when you have to testify. Once you have gained some experience as a witness, you will have much less anxiety the next time you need to make a courtroom appearance.

Be sure to call the courthouse and the attorney who subpoenaed you the day you are scheduled to testify. Refer to the case number on your subpoena to see if any schedule changes have been made. If not, report to the courthouse as instructed, and on time.

Testifying ineffectively could result in the dismissal of a case by a judge if he or she finds your testimony to be inaccurate or untruthful. Inaccurate or untruthful testimony may result in either an unjust conviction or acquittal. And, of course, should it be determined that you purposely lied under oath, you may be prosecuted for perjury.

Courtroom conduct becomes part of your overall effectiveness. Courtesy and respect are essential ingredients of your courtroom behavior. The judge is addressed as, "Your Honor." Attorneys will challenge and question you. This is their job. Your job as a witness is to be patient and answer their questions as accurately as you are able. Dress properly in business attire and in a conservative fashion. Trials are serious business and humor is generally not appropriate. When you answer questions directed to you, speak clearly and naturally and to the jury. Being courteous and respectful toward the jury as well as other courtroom personnel will result in your winning their trust and making you an effective witness.

Consider being a witness as participating in one form of an interview, and take steps to prepare yourself for this task. Prior to taking the witness stand, review any statements or depositions you may have made. It is not unusual for several months to elapse between the time a statement is made and the time when a person actually testifies. You will want to be consistent in your testimony. Go over the information in your mind; refresh your memory so you will be confident about the events and facts. If you wish, you may go over your testimony with the attorney who subpoenaed you prior to appearing in court.

Once you are on the witness stand stay calm, be courteous, and answer the questions as directly as possible with a "yes" or "no." Do not add information unless you are asked to do so. If you do not understand the question, ask to have it rephrased or repeated. If you do not know the answer to a question, simply say so. Try not to rush your answers. Take your time to give complete answers and if an attorney objects to a question, wait until the judge tells you what to do before answering it. Avoid using expressions such as, "I think" or "I feel" or "Maybe it could have been." If you become confused or unsure of what to say, you can ask the judge for a short break. An effective witness is one who stays cool under pressure no matter what questions an attorney may use to intimidate or make him or her angry. Always keep in mind that when you testify, much the same as any interview, information is being given for a specific purpose. In the case of testifying, the information is used to determine the guilt or innocence of the accused.

Hiring and Promotion

We now turn our attention to the selection process for Criminal Justice personnel. You should be aware that the more progressive states are increasing their standards. Not only are mental and physical tests required, but structured interviews are usually given to the applicants. Some states use tests made up of multiple choice items over departmental policy and procedures to test the applicant's ability to read and comprehend the type of material he or she will be expected to understand on the job. In many states this is a Civil Service examination. For Corrections, some states also require a minimum number of college credit hours to have been completed or be in the process of being taken in specific areas such as Corrections, Criminal Justice, Psychology, Sociology, Educational Psychology, Guidance and Counseling. The hours required vary from state to state, but the direction is toward more college level education for employees.

Only those applicants scoring above a predetermined score continue through the selection process. Prior to any interview, a verification of education is made through the submission of official transcripts by the applicants. Criminal history information must also be provided. If any falsification occurs, the applicant is eliminated from consideration for hire. Only after these steps have been completed will the applicant receive a notice of the date and location of an interview. It is not unusual for interviews to have both a written and oral portion. Some states permit the applicant more than one chance to pass the interview step in the selection process. The actual employment interview may vary from state to state, but there are certain steps and procedures that occur in almost any interview that an applicant may study and prepare for prior to the actual interview itself.

The point was made earlier that you should consider an interview as an opportunity for the exchange of information for a particular goal or objective. The objective in interviewing a person is to determine the applicant's areas of knowledge, skill and ability, and personal characteristics that are related to job success for the position. With this in mind, we can examine the kind of questions that you may be asked and the reasons behind them.

Structured interviews usually begin with the person leading the interview team explaining the purpose of the interview and giving the applicant the chance to ask questions about the process. Most interviewers will spend some time establishing rapport with the interviewee and attempt to put the applicant at ease. It is impossible to anticipate every question or follow-up question that you may be asked. It is possible to predict the general areas of concerns and the kind of information the interviewers are after.

Closed-Ended, Open-Ended, and Probing Questions

There are different types of questions that are used during the interview process. *Closed-ended* questions usually answered by either a yes or no answer. A few examples would be, "Is that your final answer?," "Did you take the sugar packets?," or "Did you graduate from college?" *Open-ended* questions require the interviewee to elaborate on a response rather than a simple yes or no. For example, "How did the fight start between you two?" or "Tell us about your five year goals." Most questions during an employment interview are open-ended, which are used to find out more about a specific subject. The third type of question is *probing*. Probing questions are those asked after you have answered an open-ended question and attempt to get more details and to expand on your first response. Probing questions try to dig much deeper and may focus on personal opinions, feelings, critical thinking skills, or for clarification. Examples of probing questions are "What eventually happened?," "What else can you tell me about the fight?," or "I'd like to hear more about your college experience?" Most probing questions begin with "What or How" because they try to elicit more detail.

Your responses need to be thoughtful and complete, but be careful not to ramble on and on. If additional information is wanted, the interviewer will probe further. You may also expect a few personal questions or even a surprise question. Questions about your future career goals may be asked to see if you have assessed your plans for the future. Questions about the position for which you are applying may be put to you to determine your knowledge about the department. You need to be informed about the job in general and the specific position for which you are applying as well as information about the agency (such as their mission, expectations). Very few of us can formulate the best answers we are capable of giving off the tops of our heads. Planning for an interview is essential and will pay dividends. This is true of any interview situation. Before we discuss specific questions you are likely to be asked, let us walk you through steps preparing you for the interview and then discuss guidelines to consider during the actual interview.

1. Be sure to arrive 15 to 20 minutes early for the interview. Allow for parking or driving problems. Also, be sure you know where you are expected to be, the interviewer's name and its correct pronunciation. Learn his or her rank or title. Do not bring a friend along for moral support.
2. Find out as much about the agency as you can. Learn about its history and future plans for growth. After all, you are applying for a position with an organization that, presumably, has growth potential and you wish to be a part of it.
3. Think about the possible questions you could be asked and at least prepare some answers in your mind. Writing them as well as thinking about them would be even better.
4. Dressing appropriately is important. Being on the conservative side is safer than wearing casual or flamboyant attire. When in doubt, and if possible, check with others who have gone through the interviewing process at the same agency. Along with appropriate dress, and almost too obvious to mention, neatness and cleanliness, or lack thereof, reveal much about an applicant.

No one can predict what interpersonal interaction will occur between the applicant and the interviewer or interviewers. But most interview situations are similar enough that we can provide some general guidelines.

You should expect to be nervous, that is normal, and is certainly better than giving the impression that the entire procedure is routine and not very important to you. Extreme nervousness is the opposite end of the scale, and you may be able to avoid this condition if you keep in mind that most interviewers want to see you as close to your real self as possible. With this in mind, they do not wish to embarrass you or put you on the defensive and will spend some time putting you at ease.

Shake hands with the interviewer or interviewers when you enter the office and greet them by rank and name if you know them. Be sure to use a firm, but not a muscleman, grip. Of course, you will not be chewing gum and, if you are a smoker, do not light up prior to the interview including in the car ride to the interview location.

Interviews for most positions are generally very structured. They want to find out as much about you as possible in a short time and find out what your perceptions are about the job you are seeking. In other words, it is an open exchange of information. There may be no right or wrong answers to some of the questions, but they will be able to determine how clear and articulate your replies are.

Let us examine some of the kinds of questions you will likely be asked either in the form presented here or in a similar form, but with the same purpose in mind.

Why do you want to become a *position title*?

Your answer to this would depend on your interest and personal reasons for applying for the job. The interviewers want to see if you are interested in the job as a career or simply as an interim position. A follow-up question might inquire about your work experience and education and whether it relates to what this new hire would need to know. If you reveal little knowledge of the position as a career, the odds are it will have a negative impact on the interviewers. This is another reason for you to examine the history and future plans of the particular agency to which you are applying.

The interviewers want to determine what you actually know about the position that you are seeking and what self-assessment you have made about your background and education that makes you believe you could be a successful candidate. Thinking carefully about these points prior to the interview will help you give realistic answers.

An important consideration is that jails, prisons, and police departments are operated in a paramilitary structure. Discipline and a daily planned routine are essential. The giving and taking of orders is necessary for the orderly and efficient running of any agency where it is absolutely necessary to ensure the security and safety of both officers and others. Being able to take and obey orders in an organization where authority is an important part of the system is an attribute interviewers would like to see demonstrated or revealed in an applicant's response.

Obviously, the world is populated with people of all races, religions, socioeconomic, and criminal backgrounds. Criminal Justice personnel are required to work in these surroundings with people of diverse backgrounds. Interviewers would like to know how applicants feel about working with socially deviant personalities of such diverse backgrounds that are probably different from anything they have experienced.

You will probably be asked some questions that have nothing to do with your basic knowledge, but are designed to see how well you are able to think on your feet and also to educate you about some of the dilemmas you may face.

Scenario-based situations are a very popular way interviewers assess your ability to understand and react to a hypothetical situation. You will need to comprehend the situation and its consequences so that you can give a reasonable answer. Remember, using good judgment should be involved in the enforcement of rules and regulations, as well as your answers. Do not fall into the trap of trying to figure out what you think the interviewers want to hear. With more than one interviewer asking you questions, it is better for you to be honest and consistent with your replies. If you are not, it will soon become obvious to those conducting the interview and will not be a positive influence toward your credibility.

The would-be employee should also appraise his or her own strong and weak characteristics and be able to articulate them with emphasis on the strong ones. All of us have weak points, having a quick temper, being a perfectionist, and so on, but to be able to recognize them in ourselves indicates the ability to control them. Interviewers are not looking for a superman or superwoman, but a person who displays common sense and a realistic attitude. The person who is not interested enough to have checked on the agency or the job indicates indifference and probably lacks a real conception of what being in criminal justice entails. If an applicant reveals a realistic conception of the workplace and situation and is expressing an interest in employment, it is a safe assumption that he or she is at least sincere and serious about getting hired.

Being able to use proper judgment in difficult situations is an attribute in any job, but it takes on even more importance in a prison environment where the wrong decision could result in a disaster. In answering the above questions, the applicant needs to reveal self-confidence and the ability to cope with stressful situations. Advanced thinking about incidents in your past that indicate your decision-making ability in such situations will make it easier for you to recall them during the interview and, thus, present more comprehensive answers to the interviewers questions.

Criminal justice operates in the public eye and very seldom is there complete agreement on issues. An applicant for any position would be well-advised to become informed on the current issues. That does not mean to imply that an applicant needs to be in full agreement with a department's position on these issues, but at least he or she should be able to converse intelligently about such issues as high-speed chases, the death penalty, sentencing guidelines, reentry, and other current newsmakers.

Many other questions could be asked during the course of an interview. The following list of questions is not exhaustive, but serves as a guide to anyone who is serious about preparing for an interview. By going over such a list, a person is able to think about and assess his or her own potential.

What do you think a person in this position does during a typical day?

Do you feel you have a personality for this type of work?

Why do you feel you can be responsible for the guarding, supervising, and participating in the treatment of prisoners?

Why do you feel you can be responsible for patrolling, questioning, and arresting suspects?

Corrections and law enforcement work are referred to as being paramilitary. Is that term familiar to you? Why do you think this system is used?

Does your background help prepare you for this type of organization? Do you think you could accept and work in a paramilitary organization? Could you conform to a grooming and dress code?

Have you had any bad experiences with individuals who have a different racial, religious, sexual, or criminal background? How did you handle the experience?

What in your work experiences, your home environment, or educational background would help you to cope with working with people of varied races, religions, and criminal backgrounds?

As an employee, you are legally obligated to report infractions of the rules and regulations by fellow employees. Do you think this is a good idea in all cases?

What would you do if you detected the odor of beer or alcohol on a fellow officer's breath knowing that one of the rules of conduct states that an officer must not report to work with such an odor on his or her breath?

Have you much knowledge from your reading or friends who work in this field of the actual conditions, type of prisoners (parolees, suspects), and situations you might face if employed with this agency?

What apprehensions or fears do you think you, or any new employee might have? And what characteristics do you possess that would help you deal with these apprehensions?

Have you ever had to make an important decision quickly and under pressure? What should you keep in mind when you have to make a quick decision?

Please tell us what major issues you are aware of where differences of opinion may exist between the public and this agency.

What are your future educational plans?

Which classes did you enjoy the most and why?

What long- and short-range goals have you set for yourself?

How are you going to achieve your goals?

Describe to me the ideal job.

What is it that you really do well?

Tell me about a weakness that you have.

How do you think others would describe you?

Why should we consider you for this position?

How do you feel you can contribute to this agency?

Give me an example where you have been under pressure.

Tell me about your work experiences.

What factors are most important to you in a job?

What kind of reference do you think your last employer will give you?

Tell us about a job that you have had and did not like.

CHAPTER 8

Report Writing

As Criminal Justice personnel, you will be presented with both the opportunity and the necessity of expressing yourself through written reports. Reports are used to document day-to-day activities as well as planning, developing, and implementing short- and long-term goals and policies. Reports are also used to record specific incidents that occur within your facility or agency. How well they are written reflects on you personally.

Three areas will be covered in this chapter. The first and most detailed is the actual writing of the report. We will begin by defining what a report is and what elements make up a report as well as what characteristics to look for in a good report. Before you begin writing any report, it is necessary that you consider the importance of the two other topics that will be examined in this chapter: observation skills and note-taking. You must be able to observe details carefully prior to making a report and you must be able to recall those details accurately. This is the reason you need to take careful notes on what you have seen or participated in while working. The longer the time lapses between the incident and writing the report, the easier it is for some of the details to be forgotten or distorted, unless notes are taken as soon as possible covering the essential information. Another essential skill to work on is becoming a keen observer of details. Many agencies incorporate tests of an applicant's ability to observe and to then recall what they saw. We will be dealing with this subject and provide you with exercises for practice later in this chapter.

Why is report writing important to you as a professional? Your report becomes your identity, Officer Smith's report, and it may be the source for inquiries from other interested persons. It is important that your reports be complete and accurate. A report must be clear enough so that all who are reading it can understand its meaning without confusion over the terminology used.

What Is a Report?

A **report** is a formal written presentation of facts. Reports such as misconduct reports, police reports, or presentence reports are considered formal while day-to-day communication (i.e., information reports, e-mails) is generally viewed as informal, but at any time could be considered formal in special situations.

Six Reasons for a Well-Written Report

A report is a specific message transmitted to a specific receiver, and establishes *a permanent record for the agency*. It must *reflect the facts and not contain opinions or personal judgments* in the actual text. If you wish or are asked to provide an opinion or judgment as the author of a report, you may accomplish this by attaching a separate supplemental page entitled "Confidential" or "Opinions and Conclusions."

Your written reports also are *subject to review by a wide variety of people* and agencies including your supervisors, the Courts, attorneys, probation/parole, and possibly the media. Not only should they be accurate, but correct in grammar and spelling.

Legal considerations must be kept in mind when writing your reports. The courts take the position that if an incident or action takes place and it has not been documented, then it did not happen. Since the report may appear in court as evidence or be read by people other than agency staff, it must reflect what actually occurred. Well-written reports may help to avoid successful litigation by inmates or suspects against yourself and your agency.

In Chapter 1 of this book, we talked about the need for a professional attitude toward your duties in the criminal justice field. To accept report writing as an integral part of your duties and to write them at the very best of your ability is certainly a sign of that professional attitude. A Correctional officer, police officer, and/or a probation/parole officer all have the responsibility to write and retain all reports as prescribed by departmental policy and procedure. In other words, your report is *a reflection on your training and character*.

Finally, written reports may ultimately ensure that *agency policies and procedures are applied consistently* and are appropriately documented. Noncompliance could result in disciplinary action or dismissal.

In Criminal Justice, you will be dealing with many types of reports. Here are some examples of types of reports that Corrections employees will be expected to prepare: information or administrative reports, incident reports, disciplinary reports, admitting and processing forms, prisoner money and property receipts, medical notations, various log entries, inspection reports, release reports, and reports for courts.

Reports also fall into various categories. Some reports that you complete will be reviewed for accuracy and completeness. Examples are commitment reports, register and admission reports, and release reports. There are also some reports that require no narrative, but must be very accurate in their completion. Count sheets, special meals received, and medical treatment received fall into this category. When reports require narratives and statements they may be either short or detailed descriptions. Probation/parole officers will write presentence reports and chronological case reports on a regular basis while police officers will deal with arrest reports.

Thus, a true professional knows how to prepare a well-written report. Since report writing will be part of your responsibilities within your employment, it is time to examine the characteristics of a well-written report.

Seven Essential Elements

In the first class journalism students take, they are told about the importance of identifying the five "W's" and the one "H" when preparing a story. The reference is to the who, what, where, when, why, and how that needs to be covered for an accurate story. In constructing a report in the criminal justice environment, another dimension is needed and we end up adding an "A" for action taken. If your report fails to include these seven essential elements, it will fall short of the needed material to be considered accurate and complete. Let's look at each one of these elements.

WHO? The report writer must ask the following questions:

Who discovered the incident?
Who reported the incident?
Who were the witnesses who saw, heard, or know who is involved?

When identifying the persons involved, it is necessary to identify suspects, prisoners, and clients by complete name and number (or other identifying labels such as driver's license number, date of birth [DOB], etc.). Staff should be identified by name and title or rank. Witnesses need to be identified by full name, DOB, and rank or title if appropriate. By identifying persons involved in this manner, it classifies who is involved for the reader, adds to your professionalism, and the titles may add to the witnesses' credibility. You also include your position, title/rank as well.

WHAT? The report writer asks the following:

What happened?
What was the offense or infraction committed?
What are the elements of the incident?
What objects were used or involved?

The "What" provides the details of the incident. It should be written in *chronological order* so that the reader understands exactly what you observed or participated in. It is important to give facts only, and not to insert your own opinion. Describe behaviors, don't label them.

WHERE? The report writer asks the following:

Where was the incident discovered?
Where were the persons involved seen?
Where were the tools or weapons obtained?
Where were the witnesses located to see the incident?

By answering the "where" questions, you are drawing a verbal picture for your reader. Be specific by identifying cellblock and cell numbers as well as the name of the area. Persons involved in the incident, especially witnesses, should be placed in a specific location in your narrative.

WHEN? The report writer needs to determine the following:

When was the infraction, incident, or violation committed?
When was the occurrence discovered?
When was the notification of the incident received?
When did staff arrive on the scene?
When did the incident end?

Exact time, if known, should be given. Otherwise use the approximate time relative to your own actions as closely as possible. If necessary, trace back your own activities to establish a time frame for determining when the incident you are reporting occurred.

HOW? The report writer needs to determine the following:

How was the offense, violation, or infraction committed?
How was the incident planned? (If it can be determined.)
How did the inmate use the weapons or tools?
How much damage was done?

When discussing the "how" of an incident, place the information in chronological order, that is, start at the beginning by telling how the situation started, how it progressed, and how it was concluded. (See Exercise 1 on organizing thoughts into chronological order at the end of the chapter.)

WHY? The report writer needs to ask the following:

Why was the violation, offense, or infraction committed?
Why was a particular weapon or tool used?
Why was a particular method employed?

It is imperative when seeking to answer the "why" and thus establish the motive of an incident, that the report writer distinguishes facts from opinions. Opinions are important, but must not be presented as facts. We will discuss the difference between fact and opinion shortly. If you are using secondhand information to answer the "why" in your report, be sure to give the original source.

ACTION TAKEN—This part of a report is often the weakest because others are often responsible for it rather than the original writer. Here are some questions you might consider.

What was the final disposition?
If referred, to whom?
If handled informally, how?
Are there other reports that need to be completed from witnesses or victims?

For each case, your report will probably be different in some aspect, but most of these elements, in one form or the other, will be necessary for your report.

Five Requirements of a Report

There are five requirements to ensure that a report is well written. As a professional, you should make sure every report you write includes these requirements. First, the report must be as *complete* as possible and include the seven essentials mentioned earlier. The report must be written in a fashion that a reader other than you or those directly involved will be able to understand the sequence of events. When the report is completed, you must sign your full name, rank and position or title, and the date of the report.

Second, a report needs to be *concise*. Conciseness means getting to the point and making every sentence count without editorializing. Do not repeat points and do not include unnecessary information that is not pertinent to the specific incident.

Third, keep your report *clear* to avoid confusion, misunderstanding, and loss of credibility. A clear report contains simple, descriptive words, and also words that are specific such as names, titles, times, and gender. Avoid exaggerating an incident and do not use jargon or buzz words even though you hear them every day.

Fourth, *correctness* of your report has a direct effect on you and your institution's credibility. Proper grammar, correct spelling, neatness, accurate and unbiased information, and actual words or phrases spoken, not paraphrases, are your responsibility when you put together your report.

And, fifth, *courtesy* and professionalism never go out of style and will help the report writer in gathering the necessary information for a good report. You need to indicate those who was or was not cooperative. Avoid stereotypes or biases about the individuals in your report, including the use of "loaded" words. These are words that carry meaning beyond their general meaning.

Fact Versus Opinion

Good report writing is based on fact, yet sometimes it is difficult to tell the difference between a fact and an opinion. ***Facts*** are statements that can be verified by direct use of our senses: seeing, touching, tasting, and smelling. Facts are points of information that we know are true from evidence and/or research. ***Opinions*** are personal views about something. Opinions may vary from one person to another on almost any idea or issue. Problems occur when you and the people around you all share the same opinion. The danger is that you may confuse what is actually opinion for fact.

For example:

1. _____ Babe Ruth hit sixty home runs in one season. (Fact)

2. _____ Babe Ruth was the greatest baseball player. (Opinion)

The first statement is factual because we can verify it. The second statement is opinion even though most of us would agree with it. The word "greatest" is evaluative and this statement is opinion.

Sometimes opinions are requested, such as a sentence recommendation in a presentence investigation. You must clearly state that it is your opinion, but it should be based on the facts obtained during the investigation. It is appropriate to say, "The facts support my opinion that . . . " or "My opinion is based on the facts from the case;" or "It is my belief that . . . "

Below are two reports to examine and analyze their conciseness. Read carefully to determine the strengths and weaknesses. Which report allows you, the reader, to have a complete understanding of the investigation?

Report #1 Investigation Report of Cell Fire

Superintendent Murray:

Per your instructions I investigated the fire in Ryan's cell with Lt. York. I can tell you now that the TV set was definitely not the cause of the fire. We looked over the entire cell area carefully and found no evidence that the TV set was involved in any way in causing the fire. We also had Mr. Cardinal take a look at the TV set and he concurs. Furthermore, we found a burned area and a cigarette butt on the shelf below the TV and some burned paper, which looks to be the remains of several empty Camel packs. The fire looks like it was set intentionally by Ryan and it is my opinion that he should be placed in administrative segregation pending the outcome of this investigation.

I looked up his record and found that he was brought up on disciplinary charges at Podunk Prison for a similar offense on May 12, 2005. He received ten days punitive segregation after being found guilty.

Keller said that the fire broke out soon after Ryan went to work, which was about 7:50 a.m. and that no other inmates were in the cell between the time Ryan left and the time the fire broke out. Keller heard the explosion, too, but Mr. Cardinal said that it probably occurred after the fire broke out and not before. After our investigation was completed, we had Keller deadlock the cell and instructed him that no one was to enter it without first contacting the Captain's Office. We also sent a memo to all supervisors on all shifts, alerting them of this and asking them to maintain the deadlock until they received clearance from you.

Respectfully submitted,
Sgt. Shay Taylor

There are several statements in this report that need to be looked at carefully. In the first paragraph, second sentence, it says "I can tell you now." Is this statement substantiated by the text? Who is Mr. Cardinal? In the first paragraph, last sentence "The fire broke out . . . " Is this information that is substantiated by the text? In the second paragraph, is the information pertinent to this report? Who is Keller? What is the significance of the explosion? Why was the report written? As you can see, there are many questions left unanswered. Now read Report #2.

Report #2 Investigation Report of Cell Fire

Superintendent Murray:

Per your instructions I co-investigated the fire in Ryan's (62005) cell with Lt. York. I understand that your basic concern is to determine whether or not the TV set in the cell (21 Cell, First Floor in G Building) was the cause of the fire. Presented here are our findings.

The fire apparently broke out yesterday morning, May 20, 2015, between 7:50 and 7:55 A.M. Corrections Officer Keller was on duty on the first floor of G Building at the time. He stated that Prisoner Ryan left the cell for work call at approximately 7:50 A.M. and that he heard an explosion within five minutes of that time. Corrections Officer Keller responded to the fire and noted that the cell door was locked and there were no other people in the area at the time.

Upon investigating, we found the cell to contain the wooden table stand involved in the fire with the TV on top and a single shelf with some items underneath. The cell also contained a foot locker, chair, bedding, and Ryan's personal items, but these were not involved in the fire.

Investigation of the stand disclosed that no part of the wooden stand itself burned more than two inches below the lower shelf. The top of the lower shelf of the stand was completely charred over three-fourths of the total area. The shelf contained the remains of a cigarette and at least four empty cigarette packages. The end of the cigarette was resting in the center of the remains of the cigarette packages. The TV set was sitting on the top shelf of the stand. The plastic case was melted and charred over approximately 30 percent of its area. The bottom of the set was neither disfigured nor charred and neither was the top of the stand. These findings seem to indicate that the fire originated on the bottom shelf and traveled upward. The TV set was unplugged when the investigation took place and Corrections Officer Keller reported unplugging it immediately after extinguishing the blaze.

Mr. Cardinal, the prison Electrician, investigated the electronics and reported that the 5A fuse for the outlet that the set was plugged into was still intact, as well as a 1/2A fuse inside the TV set itself. He also said that the components inside the set had soot on them, but showed no signs of burning. His findings suggested that the TV set was not the cause of the fire. He also explained that the large crack in the picture tube was probably caused by the heat of the fire and most likely produced the explosion heard by Corrections Officer Keller.

In summary, our findings indicate that the TV set in the cell at the time was not the cause of the fire. Furthermore, the fire did not appear to be the work of another prisoner, although the cause of the blaze appears to be suspicious. I recommend that this matter be investigated further.

After our investigation was completed, we had Corrections Officer Keller deadlock the cell and instructed him that no one was to enter it without first contacting the Captain's Office. We also sent a memo to all supervisors on all shifts alerting them to maintain the deadlock until they received clearance from you.

Respectfully submitted,
Sgt. Shay Taylor

Are the events in Report #2 clearer than Report #1? To decide whether or not Report # 2 is complete, let's examine how close the report writer came to answering the seven essential questions for each report. Ask yourself who was involved? What happened? When did the incident occur? Where did the incident occur? How did it happen? Why did it happen? What action was taken?

Observation

A considerable amount of time has been spent discussing what you need to include in your reports. Of course, there are times when you will not be able to write your report immediately after an incident. Medical emergencies may require immediate transportation of personnel or fire emergencies may require evacuation. Or there may be insufficient time to complete reports prior to the end of your shift. It becomes apparent that as an officer, unless you have a fantastic memory, you need to record the facts of a situation in a notebook as soon as possible until such time when the official report can be written.

Prior to note-taking, an officer must learn to be a *keen observer* of the scene and the situation. This is not a skill that simply happens overnight. A police officer who observes action occurring on a street corner will "see" much more than a layman who has not learned to pick out and remember what he or she observes. During the interview process, many agencies use short video tapes to see how much a candidate for a position is able to observe and retain. Pictures of a scene may be shown for a short time and the job candidate will be asked to recall as much of the scene as possible. Often very specific questions will be asked. At the end of this chapter, there are three activities that will give you some practice in checking your observational skills. You may also practice honing these skills by looking at a scene in a magazine or a newspaper for a few minutes and then writing everything you can recall. Try sitting in a parking lot or waiting in line at a movie and concentrate on the details around you. As you teach yourself to pay attention to details, you will be able to recall more and more after a single observation. The more accurate you become with your observational skills, the more specific details you will be able to record in your notebook for inclusion in your final report.

Note-taking

Note-taking is a critical part of the everyday world of the Criminal Justice professional. In a very real sense, your notebook is the same as evidence and should be preserved carefully. The preservation of all evidence and its careful handling should be conducted "by the book." Learn your department's or agency's policies and procedures and follow them exactly. You should implement the following standard procedures as part of the reporting process.

1. Always carry a notebook.
2. Number the pages consecutively.
3. Do not remove any pages from the notebook.
4. Record only facts and observations, not opinions; opinions are separate from notes about facts.
5. Your notes should cover the seven essentials of a report: who, what, when, where, why, how, and action taken.
6. Notes should be made as quickly as possible following the incident.
7. Notes should include verbal statements of participants and witnesses.
8. If applicable, include sketches of the scene and locations of people and important objects.
9. Be sure to note all evidence collected and its disposition. You may need to have pictures taken to identify objects and to also make notes about them.
10. Record events in chronological order and give approximate times when possible.
11. When your notebook is full, do not discard it. Keep all used notebooks in a safe place and file it in chronological order. It may be needed months or even years after the time the notes were taken.

Evidence

Any evidence obtained must also follow a standard procedure, and should be described in your notes. Make sure you know your department's policy. First, physically mark the evidence by attaching a tag or label to it. Store it in a marked container and plastic bag if applicable. Be sure it is permanently identifiable. Tags may become smudged if written on with the wrong kind of ink. Second, make a note of who assisted you in marking the evidence. Be sure to record the physical description and include such details as serial number, model number, other numbers, or names. Third, all evidence and its disposition should be recorded on the appropriate reporting forms. Finally, when evidence passes from one person to another, be sure to tell how it was secured by each person. This is called the "chain of evidence" and is required legally to show how the evidence was preserved. This is for your own protection. Mishandling or loss of evidence may result in losing a court case.

Log Entries

Due to its routine nature, one area that many officers do not take as seriously as they should deal with log entries. This duty is usually performed by line personnel and serves a vital role in documentation of the daily routine. An entry should reflect accurately the actual observations of the officer. Any and all unusual occurrences should be noted. Remember that log entries can be used in courtroom proceedings to show whether policies and procedures were followed. Thus, make sure your entries are professional and summarize what you observed or have actually done. Give enough detail so that others reading your entries know what occurred. Refrain from doodling on the log or writing personal opinions. These may come back to haunt you!

Bad Habits to Avoid

1. Imitating other writers' styles.
    You have been told what goes into a report and why it needs to be easy to read and understand. Too many beginning report writers try to imitate a "standard" style of reports they may have read from other officers. When you attempt to copy the reporting style of others or when you decide to show your creativity in reports, you are going to create confusion rather than clarity. Your purpose is to inform accurately and concisely. Try to be yourself and write in clear language. Your reports will be much more readable and factual, and in the long run, easier to write.

2. Confusing information or labels
    Certain bits of information are going to be necessary for every report filed. You need, as pointed out earlier, to give the date, time, location, and identities of all involved. Once you have completed this and this is often done in the standard heading or in the first paragraph of your report, some authors believe it is not necessary to repeat it again. Many times report writers try to present the same information, but with a different spin. For example, the writer first identifies the location as Dayroom A-6, which is factual and conveys a specific message. In an effort not to repeat the same language, the officer may refer to it as the "dayroom activity area" or the

"table area," which become confusing to the reader. The proper identification is necessary throughout the report. It would be correct to state Dayroom A-6, near the activity area, which clarifies a specific area within the dayroom.

Report writers can also confuse their readers by using words such as 'subject," "victim," or "witness." Once you have identified or labeled the players in your report, it is much easier and clearer to simply identify them by last name, unless two or more share a last name. If there are shared names, use full names (first and last name) in the rest of your narrative.

Another bad habit some report writers commit is the numbering of the subjects in their reports (Suspect #1, Victim #2, Witness #3, etc.). Using last names will do the job much more effectively and is easier for both you, as the writer, and your reader in his or her understanding of who is doing what.

Confusion also occurs when one sentence identifies the subject as Emily Jones and Kristi Smith. The next sentence uses a pronoun she, but does not state which "she." Throughout the report, make sure the reader knows who you are referring to.

3. Using vague or wordy sentences

First, if you have a number of things told to you by the same person, rather than starting four or five sentences with his or her name, it is easier to state: Crosby said, "Smith pushed Johnson, Johnson pulled a knife, Smith fell to the floor, and Johnson fled." In other words, condense what one person said into brief sentences rather than several longer sentences and paragraphs. Be specific and concise.

Many times writers think it makes them look intelligent and educated if the use bigger or more complex words. Although the words are correct, many times they are less precise and leave the reader open to interpret what the writer means. Thus, smaller words may be more exact in their description. Look how easy it is to eliminate these less precise and often ambiguous words from your reports:

"McMillan <u>indicated</u> that he did not wish to be taken into custody."

The word "indicate" is much too vague and needs to be more explicit. For example:

"McMillan yelled, "Get outa here, I'm not moving!"

If you are not this specific, your report may be considered "conclusionary," that is, you are arriving at a conclusion rather than being factual.

Several other words are just as vague. Here are a few examples:

Do not write:	**Write:**
The officer was **contacted** at his home.	I **phoned** Officer Jones at his home.
I **responded** to the call for help.	I **ran** to help Officer Griffith.
I **proceeded** to conduct an investigation.	I **investigated** . . .
I **observed** that there was a knife under the bunk.	I **saw** a knife under the bunk.

I **detected** the odor of smoke in the cell.	I **smelled** smoke in the cell.
It should be noted that the trunk was full of bottles.	**The trunk** was full of bottles.

For whatever reason, many people writing reports feel they will sound more professional by padding their reports with useless verbiage. Stick to the facts, keep it simple, and get it said. Always use specific words or terms. General words will lead to more questions.

General statement:
It was determined that Taylor was a minor.
(You are left asking, "How was it determined?")

Specific statement:
A birth certificate showed Taylor's DOB as 5-23-06.
You should not conclude that being specific always means you will be able to be brief. You will, however, be able to work toward clarity and less verbiage by substituting the suggested words for the words or phrases we have listed here.

Use the word **"said"** instead of related, explained, articulated, or verbalized.

Use the word **"told"** instead of informed, advised, notified, or instructed.

Use the word **"fight"** instead of altercation, mutual combat, or physical confrontation.

Use the word **"argument"** instead of verbal altercation, verbal dispute, heated debate, fiery exchange of words, or verbal flare-up.

Use the word **"about"** instead of regarding, in regard to, or reference.

Use the word **"because"** instead of due to the fact that, in view of the fact that, or in light of the fact that.

Use the word **"then"** instead of at this point, at this time, at which time, or at this point in time.

Use the word **"use"** instead of utilize, make use of, or employ.

Use the word **"watched"** instead of kept under observation, maintained surveillance over, or visually monitored.

The key to selecting the best word is to be factual and specific and use everyday language, not language to try to impress the reader with your vocabulary. Use personal pronouns "I" and "me," instead of "this officer," "the undersigned," "this writer," and so on.

Do not write:	**Write:**
This officer verbally advised Leigh to give to this officer the pen.	I told Leigh to give me my pen.

4. Using a *passive* voice

   Reports should be written using an "active voice," which makes the meaning of your actions clear. When using an active voice, the sentence shows what action is expressed and is more concise. Further, active sentences usually use less words and let the reader know what the subject is doing. Always use the first person to identify yourself. Many years ago, reports used passive language such as "this writer" or "this officer," which always led to confusion of who "this officer" really was. Today, we identify ourselves by using the pronoun "I."

Do not write:	**Write:**
Jackson was arrested by me. (Passive)	I arrested Jackson. (Active)
A knife was found in Inmate Weber's right boot by this officer. (Passive)	I found a knife in Weber's right boot.

5. Using jargon

   Jargon is defined as "A special language belonging exclusively to a group. It is often unintelligible to those out the group that uses it" (Dictionary.com, 2019). Oftentimes, in criminal justice, we develop language shortcuts for words used often. For example, instead of saying presentence investigation report, Criminal Justice personnel refer to it as a PSI. But outside our field, it may be the name of a company, such as "Population Services International," or it could be a mathematical shortcut for "pounds per square inch." Inmates also have their own jargon that oftentimes is picked up and used by Correctional officers. One facility placed all juveniles in yellow jumpsuits, which led to the juveniles being called "ducks." Since criminal justice reports are seen and read by outsiders, jargon and abbreviations become very confusing and may change the meaning of the message you are trying to convey. For example, it would be quite confusing for a journalist to read "The duck was out of place" rather than "The juvenile was out of place." The journalist may wonder why ducks are inside a jail.

6. Mistakes or missing information

   Ultimately, this chapter is trying to prevent you from writing a report that may be dismissed or result in litigation. Mistakes or missing information many times is grounds for dismissal. For example, writing the inaccurate time, place, or participants listed in your report, allows lawyers and opening to discredit the information. If you do not include all the essential elements in your report, you may have holes in the "story" that make the total picture incorrect. Poorly written reports that have mechanical and grammatical errors may require you to spend more time and effort rewriting the report for your supervisor. If your supervisor does not catch your mistakes, then your poorly written report damages your reputation as a professional.

   Thus, reports must be informative and specific, not vague and wordy. They must be factual and direct, clear, and accurate. Follow the suggestions we have given you in this chapter and within a short time you will find yourself writing better reports with less effort.

Activity 1: Observation

Study the picture below for 30 seconds. Memorize as many details about the scene as possible. After you have spent the allotted time, turn to the next page and answer the questions. Do not look back until you have completed all of the questions.

Source: Nancy Hogan (2016).

Answer the following questions based on your 30-second observation of the desk top scene. Read all of the possible answers carefully before circling your answer. When you have finished, look at the scene once again and see how well you did.

1. Name as many items as possible.

   _____
   _____
   _____

2. How many note pads were in the picture?
   A. One item
   B. Two items
   C. Three items
   D. Four items

3. What shapes were on the mug?
   A. Hearts
   B. Diamonds
   C. Squares
   D. No shapes
4. What color was the tape dispenser
   A. Black
   B. Gray
   C. Blue
   D. White
5. What way are the items in the pencil holder facing?
   A. Up
   B. Down
   C. Both up and down
6. What was the topic being discussed on the laptop?
   A. Tobacco
   B. Inequality
   C. Private prisons
   D. Taxes
7. What animal is in the center of the picture?
   A. Bird
   B. Cat
   C. Dog
   D. Pig
8. How many computer-related items are on the desk?
   A. Three
   B. Four
   C. Five
   D. Six
9. What was the design on the pencil holder?
   A. Bulldog
   B. Skeleton
   C. Landscape
   D. Handcuffs
10. Was there a pair of scissors in the picture?
    A. Yes
    B. No

Activity 2: Observation

Study the picture below for 30 seconds. Memorize as many details about the scene as possible. After you have spent the allotted time, turn to the next page and answer the questions. Do not look back until you have completed all the questions.

Source: Nancy Hogan (2016).

Answer the follow questions based on your 30-second observation for the office supplies scene. Read all of the possible selections carefully before answering. When you have finished, look at the scene once again and see how well you did.

1. How many pencils were in the picture?
   A. One pencil
   B. Two pencils
   C. Three pencils
   D. Four pencils
2. How many pens were in the picture?
   A. Four pens
   B. Five pens
   C. Six pens
   D. Seven pens

3. What color was in the background?
   A. Pink
   B. Blue
   C. Yellow
   D. Orange

4. How many silver thumbtacks were on the desk?
   A. 14
   B. 18
   C. 22
   D. 25

5. What was the name on the black eraser?
   A. Expo
   B. Bic
   C. Zippo
   D. Parker

6. Other than paperclips, how many paper clasps were in the picture?
   A. None
   B. One
   C. Two
   D. Three

7. What two objects in the picture are not considered office supplies?

   _____

8. What color was the dot on the scissors?
   A. Blue
   B. Red
   C. Black
   D. Green

Activity 3: Observation

In this next exercise, spend 30 seconds reading the following passage. As you read it, count the number of "F's" in the passage. Remember to go through the passage only once.

> **The finished files are the result of four years of scientific study combined with the five years of experience.**

How many "F's" did you find? Try it once more and see if you are able to find a few more. Most people miss a few even when looking very carefully. We may become more proficient observers through practice and concentration upon details. These skills are very important skills to possess as a Correctional officer. Thus, a true professional knows how to prepare a well-written report. Since report writing will be part of your responsibilities within your employment, it is time to examine the characteristics of a well-written report.

Reference

Jargon. (2019). *Dictionary.com*. Retrieved from https://www.dictionary.com/browse/jargon

CHAPTER 9

Common Reports Written by Criminal Justice Professionals

Students returning from internships are shocked by the amount of paperwork required by all branches of the criminal justice system. The criminal justice field is scrutinized by the public and any deviation from what is expected may result in a lawsuit. Thus, agencies require documentation to ensure employees follow policies and procedures.

Depending on the level of government, agencies may differ in types of forms and the procedures to follow. For example, local jurisdictions will differ the most, while state agencies will all have similar expectations. Thus, state probation/parole officers will be required to use the same forms no matter where they reside. This is also true of federal agencies. On the federal level, forms and procedures will be consistent from state to state. The following is a general overview of more common reports seen in criminal justice.

Log/Activity Sheets/Chronologicals

Accountability of worker activities is paramount to ensure that an agency runs smoothly. One way to track the activities of individual workers is through the use of *logs/activity sheets*. These documents show your activity noting the date and time that an action or observation occurs and how you responded. Even though these sheets are used internally to indicate daily activity, they have the potential to become public documents used to assess proper handling of incidents that occur on the job. Many times they are used in lawsuits and can protect a worker who is being accused of not performing specific duties. Of course, they can also be used to show that a worker was negligent in performing his or her job. The log is considered a permanent record and can be used to examine past actions, to pass on information to others, to help with investigations, to document behavior, to prepare court cases, to evaluate activities, and to evaluate your performance. Thus, completion of daily log sheets is an essential requirement of criminal justice.

In Corrections, the log sheet should reflect standard requirements of your job (i.e., cell checks), any problems that are out of the ordinary (i.e., maintenance issues), observations of others (i.e., people arguing), calls and requests from control, movement of inmates (i.e., medical), periodic counts, and any actions performed by you.

In law enforcement, logs serve the same function. The log sheet should reflect the standard requirements of your position, calls from dispatch, your response, any contact with citizens, and the action taken (i.e., traffic stop) as well as any observations or suspicious behavior you encounter. In departments with more advanced computer systems, the traditional log sheet has become obsolete as the computer generates a list of officer activities each day.

Each entry should include time of occurrence, specific actions, names of all involved, and your response. Some agencies also require you to initial your entries. Since this is a permanent record, the logs must be written in pen, preferably black ink. The entries should be based on fact and not your opinion. Describe unusual behavior, but do not label it (i.e., Do not state the inmate is crazy). Finally, the entries should be clearly written and as professional as possible.

Chronological reports are used by probation/parole and agencies that supervise or counsel offenders. These documents summarize the interactions between the worker and the client. Date and time should be stated with a brief explanation of the interaction. For example, if the court requires the client to attend retail theft class, the probation officer would set up a time and date for the client to participate. The communication with the retail theft class should be documented. Then, when the probation officer informs the client that he must attend this class and gives him the location and time of the meeting, it should be documented as well. The entries should be brief, but should avoid initials or shorthand that others may not understand. As with most documents, these become permanent records and may be used in court procedures, such as revocation hearings. They are also helpful to workers who have large caseloads. A brief overview of past entries can update a worker on the status of their client.

Presentence Investigations

Presentence investigations (PSI) are reports compiled by field service workers. In Michigan, PSI reports must be completed for all felony convictions. The judge or district court magistrate may also order the completion of a PSI for misdemeanor charges. A defendant may also request the completion of a PSI at the misdemeanor level, but the judge makes final decision of whether it is completed. These documents not only aid the court in determining a sentence, but are used by Corrections to decide custody and security level as well as programming needs. Once a person is released on parole, parole officers also use the PSI to follow-up on specific problem areas that continue to need to be addressed (i.e., drug treatment).

There are certain legal and court-directed requirements that form the basic structure of the PSI. The legal requirements include that the evaluation is based on facts, inclusion of a victim impact statement if requested by the victim, a written recommendation based on the evaluation, in cases of consecutive sentencing inclusion of statements from the prosecuting attorney, and diagnostic opinions that are available. The Michigan Court rules dictate the information must be researched and verified by the probation officer. These include the following areas:

- Prior criminal convictions and juvenile adjudications
- Description of the current offense and the circumstances surrounding it
- Vocational background and work history (including military record)
- Social history including marital status, financial status, educational background, length of residence in community, and other important information
- Medical history, substance abuse history, and if needed, a current psychological/ psychiatric report
- Victim information including financial, social, psychological, or physical harm suffered. Restitution needs are included
- If requested, a written victim's impact statement
- Defendant's statement
- Prosecutor's statement on any consecutive sentencing provisions
- Evaluation of defendants adjustment to community
- A recommendation for disposition
- Any other information that could help the court in sentencing (Michigan Department of Corrections, 2012)

Depending on the circumstances, the court can order the full investigative report, an abbreviated PSI, or informal request for an oral report. Each section of information is collected through interviews and record checking. Sections that are not verified for accuracy should state so. At the end of the investigation, the probation officer makes a recommendation based on the facts obtained in the case. The primary purpose of the PSI is to provide the sentencing court with timely, relevant, and accurate data to identify the most appropriate sentencing alternative and correctional disposition. The report serves five functions:

1. Aid Courts in determining an appropriate disposition
2. Assist prisons in classification, assignment to institutional programs, and release planning
3. Furnish the parole board with information pertinent to the case and aid in the decision-making process for parole consideration
4. To aid probation/parole officers in the supervision and treatment efforts
5. To serve as a source of information for research

The PSI tries to give an understanding of the offender from several points of view. It describes the defendant's character and personality, evaluates his or her needs, helps to understand the world where the defendant lives as well as the relationships he or she has with others. Overall, the PSI tries to look at both internal and external factors that may contribute to the person's deviancy.

Most presentences contain the following information:

1. Offense   The defendant's version, any statements by codefendants, statements of witnesses, statements of victims, and the official police report
2. Prior record   Adult arrests and convictions, juvenile record

3. Personal   Demographic information about the defendant, such as parents, siblings, marital status, children, where lives, education, work history, health (physical and mental), military service, and financial conditions (assets and liabilities)

4. Evaluation   Sentencing options, treatment needs
5. Recommendations   Summary of information and evaluation

Major and Minor Misconducts

In any prison system, there are specific rules that must be followed by the inmates. These rules define what specific prison behavior is prohibited and what is subject to disciplinary action. It is essential that the Corrections personnel be familiar with these violations.

The objective of a prisoner disciplinary process is to provide the institution a means of maintaining order and enforcing necessary rules within facilities. It also ensures that prisoners are provided with fair, timely, and an impartial disposition of charges that allege violations of rules. These procedures are based on state and federal statutes, administrative rules, and due process requirements for disciplinary matters.

In most facilities, alleged violations of written rules are classified as "major misconducts" or "minor misconducts." Misconduct reports may be written only for the violations that are on the list.

The structure of the disciplinary process is one of progressive sanctions. The least drastic method to ensure prisoner compliance with the rules should be used. Counseling should be attempted to correct minor violations. However, when new infractions require a more formal resolution, a misconduct report may be written. When a misconduct report is written, it must be prepared as soon as possible after the violation is observed or reported. Since the possible sanctions are more severe for major misconducts, greater procedural safeguards are provided for those charged with such violations. Prisoners have such rights as (a) advanced written notice of the charge, (b) a hearing before an impartial hearing officer, (c) to be present at the hearing if they choose, (d) the right to request witness statements and supporting documents, (e) the right to a timely hearing, and (f) the right to appeal the hearing officer's final decision. If found guilty of a misconduct, prisoners may lose privileges, serve detention time (locked in their cell), be placed in segregation, be transferred to a higher security level facility, and possibly forfeit good time from their sentence.

The Michigan Department of Corrections is unique in that it refers to certain violations as nonbondable, meaning the inmate automatically is placed in temporary segregation until seen by the hearing officer. Bondable violations mean the inmate does not have to go to temporary segregation, unless the shift commander deems it necessary for safety and security reasons. Thus, the shift commander can "revoke bond." MDOC also provides a detailed misconduct book for personnel to follow. In it, there are three other kinds of disciplinary charges possible: accomplice, attempt, or conspiracy to commit a specific violation. Immediately following is a list and/or definition of the violation and then in the first subheading, a typical example is provided. The next subheading, "Officer," describes those elements that the staff member must cover in the misconduct report for the conduct to fit the charge. The third subheading is titled "Hearing Officer" and the elements are listed that the hearing officer must find present to substantiate a finding of guilt. Certain violations require physical evidence for a guilty finding and these are marked as well.

For most facilities, an employee handbook and the inmate handbook clearly spell out what is considered a major or a minor misconduct. It is the officer's responsibility to determine the who, what, where, when, and why of the rule infractions. Probably the single biggest mistake made by new officers is the use of "conclusionary statements." An example of this for the misconduct charge of fighting would be an officer writing "I observed these two prisoners fighting." This is a conclusionary statement because it concludes something without sufficient information for the hearing officer to actually determine if a fight occurred. The reporting officer has already made this assumption, but did not provide information to back up his observation. A better statement by the Reporting Officer would be "I saw Prisoner Jones and Prisoner Smith fighting. Jones struck Smith in the face several times with a clenched fist. Prisoner Smith then kicked Prisoner Jones twice in the groin area." The reporting officer needs to be specific in his or her comments.

Critical Incidents

The Michigan Department of Corrections requires in the more serious prison incidents that a "critical incident" report be written. This would include incidents such as stabbings, homicides, escapes, serious employee misconduct, firing of a weapon, riots, fires, and sexual assaults. These events are immediately reported by telephone to the Central Office, but then are followed up with a detailed written critical report including evidence, signed statements of staff involved or witnesses, and video or pictures, if applicable. The report is compiled by the shift commander and must be completed before leaving work the day of the incident. Many times these incidents are reported to the media.

The report includes specific policy requirements and addresses compliance or noncompliance in the handling of the incident. As an example, in a stabbing that may include a kitchen knife, the report would address how the kitchen knife security procedures were followed or if they were not.

A postincident review by the Warden and/or Central office staff is always completed in such incidents. This review is to identify, assess, and correct any problem areas noted. This review may also mandate follow-up investigation, policy/procedure changes, employee discipline, and so on. This review also critiques the critical incident report to ensure it contains:

1. A detailed description of the sequence of events; to include date, time, and location of events
2. Written, signed statements from all witnesses and employees involved in the incident
3. Documents pertinent to the incident such as videos, photos, copies of applicable policies, and so on
4. Supervisory review and signatures

Law Enforcement Arrest Reports

Arrest reports are the "entry" document into the criminal justice system. They will be viewed by every agency, from supervisors to prosecutors and defense attorneys, judges, appellate courts, corrections, and finally, probation/parole departments. Thus, it is critical for the officer to carefully write the report using clear and concise language, but also to have correct grammar and spelling. Most agencies have forms with boxes that require specific information such as the officer's name and badge number of the reporting officer; the date, time, and location of the event; the specific offense and corresponding criminal code number; and the names, date of births, addresses, and telephone numbers of those involved. Many reports use initials to denote whether or not the person is the complainant, the victim, a witness, and so on. Other preliminary information may include information about a vehicle and other officers who have responded.

The report should contain the observations and actions of those involved, statements from victims/witnesses/suspects, any investigation done at the scene, evidence collected, and the disposition of the case (i.e., arrest and detention). The elements of the crime must be addressed with all legal requirements being met. For example, if the officer searches a vehicle, the report should state what led up to the search (probable cause). In the narrative, most agencies use last names to identify who is doing what, but follow your agency's policy.

The Michigan State Police have compiled a Report Writing Handbook that provides detailed information that should be contained in a report. Although, not required by county and city jurisdictions, it is a nice guide to writing a good report. The handbook provides the necessary subheadings that should be addressed in the report. For most offenses, the common subheadings are the following:

- Information—a summary of the events
- Venue—exact location including city, township, and county
- Date and time—includes day of the week
- Victim—full name, race, sex, date of birth, physical description, address, phone number, driver's license number, and social security number of the victim
- Interview with Victim/Complainant—this section should be clear and concise based on statements made and questions asked
- Suspect—full name, race, sex, date of birth, physical description, address, phone number, driver's license number, and social security number of the victim
- Suspect's statements—this section should be clear and concise based on statements made and questions asked
- Arrest—details who was arrested, for what, and their disposition (lodged in County Jail, released on own recognizance (ROR)
- Advise of Rights—this should state specifically who read the arrestee his or her rights, date and time, location, and whether the suspect waived these rights

Based on the specific crime, other subheadings may be used such as traffic stop, vehicle search, evidence collected, investigation, damaged property, scene.

Subheadings not only help the officer address specific legal requirements, but make the report easier to understand and follow.

Use of Force

The use of force is a necessary element used by Criminal Justice personnel to accomplish legitimate objectives (American Correctional Association [ACA], 1987; Hemmons & Altherton, 1999; Henry, 1994; Hogan, 1996). A clear distinction is made between appropriate use of force and excessive use of force. "Force that is legally permissible is force that is reasonable and necessary at the time of the incident" (ACA, 1987, p. 58). Two factors define reasonable force "1) the circumstances under which the force is used, and 2) the amount of force employed" (Silverman, 2001, p. 361). Thus, legitimate force involves how a reasonable officer defines conflict and uses the necessary amount of force needed to gain control (Hemmons & Altherton, 1999).

For Corrections, to ensure that the institutional goals of security are met, the ACA identifies the following justifiable circumstances where force may be applied: (a) to maintain or regain control, (b) when there is imminent danger of injury to persons, (c) serious damage to property, or (d) to prevent escape. To maintain order, force may also be used "1) to overcome an inmate's physical resistance to a lawful command, 2) to restrain an inmate when ordered to allow medical treatment, and 3) to change the location of an inmate" (Henry, 1994, p. 10). For policing agencies, the scope is a little narrower. According to the National Institute of Justice (2019), use of force for law enforcement is permitted to "mitigate an incident, make an arrest, or protect themselves or others from harm" (para. 3).

Most agencies have developed a use-of-force continuum, which summarizes the appropriate response based on a subject's actions. The Subject Control continuum was designed to help reduce potential injury to both the staff and the subject, as well as reduce use of force complaints and liability. A well-written report becomes the best defense against claims regarding excessive use of force. Certain elements should be contained within the report. First, a description of the subject's actions and the officer's (your) responses should be recorded. The subject's actions follow an escalating continuum beginning with inactive resistance, passive resistance, active resistance, active aggression, and ending with deadly force assault. Your response should be based on the subject's actions. These responses also follow an escalating continuum beginning with your presence and verbal direction, compliance controls, physical controls, intermediate controls, and ending with deadly force. If the subject de-escalates his or her behavior, your response should also reflect deescalation. Your report should explain the "totality of circumstances." You should make sure that you discuss all the facts and circumstances that confront you that lead to the use of force. Anyone that is involved in the incident must be listed in the report. You should get statements from these witnesses. Also, make sure you include any injuries that occur to anyone involved. These should be documented by medical staff. Are any weapons used? Was the incident videotaped? These should be stated in the report, labeled, and placed into evidence. Remember, a detailed, high-quality report can prevent unnecessary challenges to the legitimacy of using force.

In conclusion, report writing is an integral part of any criminal justice position. Although we have only touched on a few reports used by different agencies, there are many types of reports that you will have to write. You should take the time to learn the fundamentals in this workbook and learn to write clearly and concisely, giving the specific information required for each type of report. Remember, part of being a professional is your writing!

References

American Correctional Association. (1987). *Legal responsibility and authority of correctional officers.* College Park, MD: Author.

Hemmons, C., & Altherton, E. (1999). *Use of force: Current practice and policy.* Upper Marlboro, MD: American Correctional Association.

Henry, P. (1994). The 1993 national survey on use of force incidents and procedures in correctional institutions. Unpublished report prepared for the American Correctional Association under the Prison Setting Field Evaluation Project, Alexandria, VA.

Hogan, N. (1996). *May the force be with you: Men and women detention officers using force.* (Unpublished doctoral dissertation). Arizona State University, Tempe, AZ.

Michigan Department of Corrections. (2012). *Pre-sentence investigation and report.* Retrieved from https://www.michigan.gov/documents/corrections/06_01_140_396739_7.pdf

National Institute of Justice. (2019). *Police use of force.* Retrieved from https://www.nij.gov/topics/law-enforcement/officer-safety/use-of-force/pages/welcome.aspx

Silverman, I. (2001). *Corrections: A comprehensive view.* Belmont, CA: Wadsworth Publishing.